Aunt Pat

Enjoy! He Has Risen!

love Katherine

MOVING

BEYOND

ANXIETY

DAVID CHADWICK

HARVEST HOUSE PUBLISHERS
EUGENE, OREGON

Cover design by Studio Gearbox

Cover Photo © Marie Maerz / Shutterstock

Moving Beyond Anxiety
Copyright © 2019 by David Chadwick
Published by Harvest House Publishers
Eugene, Oregon 97408
www.harvesthousepublishers.com

ISBN 978-0-7369-7846-0 (pbk)
ISBN 978-0-7369-7847-7 (eBook)

Library of Congress Cataloging-in-Publication Data

Names: Chadwick, David (David Egbert), author.
Title: Moving beyond anxiety / David Chadwick.
Description: Eugene, Oregon : Harvest House Publishers, [2019]
Identifiers: LCCN 2019034726 (print) | LCCN 2019034727 (ebook) | ISBN
   9780736978460 (trade paperback) | ISBN 9780736978477 (ebook)
Subjects: LCSH: Anxiety—Religious aspects—Christianity. |
   Worry—Religious aspects—Christianity. | Trust in God—Christianity.
Classification: LCC BV4908.5 .C39 2019 (print) | LCC BV4908.5 (ebook) |
   DDC 248.8/6—dc23
LC record available at https://lccn.loc.gov/2019034726
LC ebook record available at https://lccn.loc.gov/2019034727

20 21 22 23 24 25 26 27 28 / VP-GL / 10 9 8 7 6 5 4 3 2 1

ACKNOWLEDGMENTS

To Marilynn, the love of my life, thank you.

To my kids and grandkids, who have loved me unconditionally, thank you.

To my friends at Moments of Hope Church for believing in me, thank you.

To Steve Miller, just a great editor and friend, thank you.

To Jesus, my Lord and Savior, thank you.

CONTENTS

PART 1:

IDENTIFYING ANXIETY

CHAPTER 1

THE BATTLE FOR YOUR MIND

Anxiety and fear are inextricably linked in life. What is the difference between these two negative emotions? Anxiety is thinking that something bad *might* happen to you. Fear is the belief that something bad *will* happen to you. When chronic anxiety persists, it inevitably leads to fear.

That is why this book focuses on anxiety instead of fear. It is my belief that if you eliminate anxiety, fear will follow. If you change the root, you'll affect the fruit. If you cut off the head of the snake, it will die.

Also, I will use the terms *anxiety* and *worry* interchangeably. The Bible seems to do the same. It also throws in the synonym *fret* as well: "Rest in the LORD and wait patiently for Him; *do not fret*" (Psalm 37:7-8 NASB).

Anxiety, worry, and fretting are all bad for you.

But let's be clear from the beginning: Anxiety is not a sin. It's an emotion. Yet it *is* an emotion that, when left unattended, can lead to sin. To terribly destructive behavior. From overeating to overindulging in alcohol or to regularly lashing out at others, anxiety can hurt your life.

But anxiety is not a sin in and of itself.

Anxious feelings *are* real. That feeling of dread can create an iciness of the soul. It's a biting wind within that won't stop screaming. And if a break does come, like the sun bursting forth in your soul after weeks of foreboding clouds, you're soon snapped back into reality. You are convinced your joy is only momentary.

Rest becomes impossible. Your energy is drained. Your peace is stolen. Your hope evaporates. You don't have energy to do daily work.

Those who attend church are not immune to the pain of anxiety. In a recent survey of 2,400 churchgoers, about 80 percent expressed that they lived with moderate to significant levels of fear.[1]

How does this fact square with the Bible's frequent commands to not succumb to fear? To be anxious for nothing?

How can you win the war with worry?

Where the Battle Rages

The battle is in your mind. It begins with how you think.

Human behavior begins with thoughts. Thoughts then produce feelings. And feelings cause behavior. To focus on feelings in an attempt to change behavior seldom has long-term success. If you do that, you will not have addressed the real reason for the undesired behavior. It's like cutting off a weed on the surface of the ground yet leaving the root untouched. The noxious weed will return.

First, you think. Then you feel. Finally, you act on your feelings.

Therefore, to change your behavior, you *must* focus on your thought life—not your feelings. Win the battle for your thought life and you will win the battle over anxiety.

Cognitive therapists preach this truth. They know that the way to change your reality is to move your mind toward rational thinking.

Reflective listening experts try first to find the patient's "feeling" words. The therapist then repeats these words to the patient and asks, "Is that what you are feeling?" If the patient says yes, the therapist then begins to help the patient discern the thoughts behind the feelings. He or she knows that a bad thought life produces bad feelings.

Alcoholics Anonymous refers to this bad thought life as "stinking thinking." Experts who deal with alcoholism know that alcoholic behavior is rooted in wrong thinking.

What the Bible Says

But long before psychotherapists arrived at this conclusion, the Bible taught it. Solomon wrote, "As he thinks in his heart, so is he" (Proverbs

23:7 NKJV). Solomon suggests that a person's life is the result of his thoughts.

The author of Job wrote, "The thing that I fear comes upon me, and what I dread befalls me" (Job 3:25). The writer concluded that much fear and dread falls upon the person whose thoughts are chronically filled with fear and dread.

Read through the following verses from Paul:

"Do not be conformed to the world, but be transformed by the renewal of your mind, that by testing you may discern what is the will of God, what is good and acceptable and perfect" (Romans 12:2). Paul believed that life transformation comes from mind information. Belief causes behavior.

"Finally, brothers, whatever is true, whatever is honorable, whatever is just, whatever is pure, whatever is lovely, whatever is commendable, if there is any excellence, if there is anything worthy of praise, think about these things" (Philippians 4:8). Paul exhorted his readers to focus their thoughts on things that would produce healthy behaviors.

"We destroy arguments and every lofty opinion raised against the knowledge of God, and take every thought captive to obey Christ" (2 Corinthians 10:5). Paul recognized that spiritual enemies are besieging your mind. To defeat them, you must take *every* thought captive. You cannot afford even one contrary thought against God to enter your mind. Not even one. It will eventually fester and become a toxic feeling that will lead to destructive behavior.

"Set your minds on things that are above" (Colossians 3:2). Paul knew that Christians are eternal creatures. This world and all its worries are not going to exist in heaven. Therefore, you must make sure that every thought in your mind is rooted in an eternal perspective. When you look at life's issues from God's view, they become increasingly small. That's what faith is—seeing life through his eyes.

Jesus taught this same truth.

He said, "What comes out of a person is what defiles him. For from within, out of the heart of man, come evil *thoughts*, sexual immorality, theft, murder, adultery, coveting, wickedness, deceit, sensuality, envy, slander, pride, foolishness. All these evil things come from within, and they defile a person" (Mark 7:20-23). Evil thoughts come from within. Then follows destructive human behavior.

Jesus said that murder begins with an angry thought (Matthew 5:21-22). Adultery begins with a lustful thought (Matthew 5:27-28). Jesus clearly taught that your thoughts affect what you do.

This perspective should empower your prayer life. How you think motivates how you pray. Positive thinking encourages faith-filled prayers. Negative thinking stimulates doubt and unbelief.

Jesus connected thinking with prayer. He said, "If you believe, you will receive whatever you ask for in prayer" (Matthew 21:22 NIV). In this verse, Jesus noted that the power of prayer begins with your thought life. Whatever you believe in your mind is what you ask the Father for, and this will eventually determine how you pray.

> **If you want victory over anxiety,
> the fight begins in the mind.**

This truth is not limited to Jesus and his followers. Even the Enlightenment thinker René Descartes understood the power of our thought life. "I think, therefore I am" was a phrase that guided his understanding of how to accrue human knowledge, which in turn would change for the better the way people lived.

If you want victory over anxiety, the fight begins in the mind. That is the battlefield. Thoughts determine feelings. And feelings lead to behavior.

Your Enemy

The enemy of your soul, the devil, knows how life works. He understands how human behavior works. And he does not want you to live in God's love and peace. He realizes that if he attacks your mind, and you believe his lies, then you'll behave in a godless, destructive way.

The enemy's strategy is to plant worrisome thoughts within your mind. Everyone knows those moments when a random, negative, fearful, or evil thought seems to come from nowhere. You ask, "Where did *that* come from?" It's from the enemy. It's how he operates. This is his strategy for luring you to disobedient behavior.

You *must* be aware of how the enemy works. He wants you to fret over your out-of-control circumstances. They surround you. They seem insurmountable. He whispers to your mind that you need to walk by sight, and not by faith (contrary to what 2 Corinthians 5:7 says). He wants to convince you that the mountains in your life can never be scaled.

The enemy earnestly throws distorted thoughts into your mind. He knows that if you chronically fix your eyes on your problems, you'll become anxious. Faith will flee, and hope won't sustain you.

Jesus called the enemy the ruler of this world (John 12:31; 14:30). Paul referred to him as the god of this world (2 Corinthians 4:4). He is a powerful foe. He has enormous wiles and superlative schemes. He doesn't take a day off. He is forever tempting you. He furiously attacks the minds of people to kill, steal, and destroy them all (John 10:10).

Satan is the father of lies (John 8:44). He has no power without his lies. He constructs situations and circumstances shrouded in half-truths and falsehoods. He encourages unbelief. If he can plant anxious thoughts in your mind, then he can move you away from faith in the Father and his truth.

It's Your Choice

But you must remember that the devil is only a tempter. That's all he can do. He cannot force people to do anything against their will.

My mom used to say, "David, you can't keep the birds from flying over your head. But you can keep them from building a nest in your hair." She was a wise woman. She knew that no one can keep bad thoughts and temptation from arising in the mind. It's a fallen world.

> God is with you—this is the reason
> all fear should flee.

While you cannot prevent the enemy from trying to plant his thoughts in your mind, you *can* choose whether you will allow him to build a nest in your hair. That is your choice, one for which *you* are responsible.

You either believe that God has every ability to meet your needs or he doesn't. You either believe that God is omniscient or he isn't. You either believe that God is present with you or he isn't.

If God isn't with you, then you *should* be anxious. Probably more anxious than you already are. The universe is full of chaos, and everything—including your life—is out of control.

But God *is* with you—this is the reason all fear should flee. And whenever the Bible says, "Do not be afraid; God is with you," it's not a stern rebuke, but a gentle reminder. God's perfect, abiding, and eternal presence overwhelms all anxiety. This peace is promised to all who trust in him.

Before Paul exhorted his readers to be anxious for nothing (Philippians 4:6-7), he began the chapter by reminding them that God was near. The promise of his presence. He oversees all. Nothing is beyond his control.

Choose to trust in his presence and promises!

In Deuteronomy 28–29, God gave to his people a list of blessings or curses that they could experience after they entered the Promised Land. The blessings are extraordinarily wonderful—from long life to fertility to strong foundations in their buildings. The curses are woefully terrible—from being overwhelmed by their enemies to food shortages to lack of rain.

But whether they received blessings or curses was up to them. It was their choice.

That's why Moses adjured them to choose life, not death (Deuteronomy 30:19). And I am convinced that Moses was saying as well, "Choose thoughts of life, not death." I think he knew that blessings and curses begin with what you think—whether your thoughts fill you with faith or anxiety.

An Illustration

Here is one way to view the battle: You have two dogs who live in your mind. One wants only what is best for you. Health. Wholeness. Peace. Love. Joy. Life. The other dog only wants your destruction. Illness. Doubt. Fear. Anxiety. Hate. Loneliness. Death.

Each day, your thoughts are like food to these two dogs. The good dog can only prosper and grow stronger with life-giving, faith-filled thoughts. The bad dog can only prosper and grow with negative and anxious thoughts. Whichever dog you feed becomes the stronger one who controls your mind.

If the good dog is fed regularly, he will eventually overwhelm and destroy the bad dog. Or vice versa. But the determining factor is the thoughts you choose to feed them each day. Thoughts that are prompted by what you read and watch. What do you permit to enter and rest in your mind? Remember: The idle brain is the devil's workshop.

You decide. It's your choice.

A Quick Review

Once again, here is Satan's strategy. He plants thoughts of worry in your mind. It's a trap. The bait is set. He wants you to fixate on the size of the issue, not the size of your God. Whatever you decide, you are inviting him and his thoughts to live inside your mind. Or not.

But the choice is entirely yours whether to take the bait or not. If you choose to focus on the lie, the trap closes. The devil cackles with delight. "Gotcha," he says. Anxiety has now become a part of your thinking—a squatter and persistent guest. And the more you dwell on how awful and challenging your problems are, the larger they will become.

You are now trapped in an ongoing cycle of unbelief. Impossibility thinking. The Lord seems distant and unable to help you in your time of need.

Never underestimate how furious this battle is. It is real and intense. The enemy is relentless in his attacks. He desperately wants to control your thought life.

Your peace of mind is at stake.

Choose Faith

Jesus invited Peter to step out of the boat in faith and walk on the water to him (Matthew 14:28). For one bold moment, Peter did. But as he looked around and saw the huge waves surging up and down all around him, his faith melted into anxiety.

Jesus rescued Peter from the raging sea, but not without a rebuke. "You of little faith, why did you doubt?" Jesus asked Peter (verse 31).

Every day of your life, Jesus invites you to dance with him on the waters of faith. To set aside all your anxieties and focus your eyes on him. To move forward in life with him. To enjoy every single second in his presence. To refuse to allow thoughts like *What if…* or *I don't know what to do* to enter your mind.

You have a choice.

But your best option still remains this: Choose to go to Jesus. Trust him with every part of your life. Refuse thoughts that distract you. Choose to fill your mind with faith in your Creator.

I once saw a bumper sticker that said, "Better dead than dread." I have come to that same conclusion: I'd rather be dead than live in dread.

Don't you feel the same way?

Anxiety saps strength from your soul. It sours life's joy. Erases its purpose. Aren't you tired of living in dread? Don't you want to be freed from its prison?

Choose Jesus. Choose faith. Know his presence.

Final Thoughts

When you choose Jesus, you know that his victory over anxiety begins in your mind. In your thought life. That's where the battle rages. And you alone control what thoughts enter, remain in, or dominate you.

It's your choice.

God doesn't want you to live in anxiety. As fear was the first negative emotion in the Bible (Genesis 3:7), rooted in the Fall, so is its first cousin anxiety. Jesus wants captives to be free. It is for freedom that Jesus came (Galatians 5:1).

That's why Jesus doesn't want your heart weighed down with anxiety (Luke 21:34). He wants you to give your burdens to him. He wants you to be free from *all* problems that weigh you down—including anxiety (Matthew 11:28-30).

In the upcoming chapter, we will look at the causes of anxiety—the problems that cause your mind to fixate on anxiety and not faith. The waves that surge around you. When you focus on them, faith cannot operate. And anxiety will only increase.

But once you identify the causes of anxiety, you can claim the cures.

And set your mind on things above.

CHAPTER 2

THE CAUSES OF ANXIETY

The battle to defeat anxiety takes place in the mind. It's won or lost there. Positive thoughts cause positive feelings. Negative thoughts prompt negative feelings. Anxious thoughts stir anxiety.

Consequently, to know the enemy's wiles is to defeat him. As Christians, we cannot be unaware of his hideous lies and schemes.

Remember: If the enemy can get you to dwell on thoughts that make your circumstances seem insurmountable, he wins. If he can get you to look at your problems and not God's promises, anxiety will blossom.

Let's look now at the kinds of circumstances the enemy uses to cause anxious thoughts to take root in your mind.

Circumstances that Cause Anxiety

Rapid Change

My wife Marilynn and I were recently watching a movie from the 1980s. The main character was fleeing villains because he had information that could destroy the USA. Those in power didn't want the information made public. So some government authorities pursued the individual with all their power.

The main character fleeing the threat had only one friend who could help him. She was always present to help him escape a seemingly hopeless situation.

At one point in the movie, it looked like the main character had been cornered. There was no way out. The bad guys were pressing in. He was desperate, searching for a solution.

That's when I blurted out to Marilynn, "This is crazy. Why doesn't he take out his cell phone and call his girlfriend? She is always there to bail him out. She could find a way to help him out of this mess."

Marilynn gave me an incredulous look. "David," she said, "the movie was made *in the 1980s!*"

Oops! Of course—there were no cell phones in the 1980s. Doesn't it seem like they have been with us forever?

Neither were laptop computers. Or smartphones. Or smart televisions. Or other technological advancements like wristwatches that notify us when to stand up and start exercising. Or record how many steps we have taken that day. Or monitor our heartbeat.

And how rapidly this change has occurred! Just as you grow accustomed to the latest gadget, it's already being updated.

Anxiety increases as you become concerned about mastering the updates—only to find out the next version is about to come out.

Instant Communication

People used to receive their news and information at certain time slots every morning or evening. Now people can watch the latest breaking news all day and night. With each proclamation of news, you can continue to worry about what is happening locally and globally 24 hours a day!

Via social media, you can now know anything everywhere immediately. If there is a tsunami in the Pacific, you will know about it right away. If a study reveals an increase in global warming, it is a headline to you within seconds. When a terrorist attack happens, it is immediately reported. One crisis after another bombards your mind.

Many people constantly fixate their thoughts on such bad news—and their anxiety increases.

No wonder there are increasing numbers of sleep disorders. More and more people are seeking sleep aids. When you go to bed and close your eyes, your mind is still overloaded with the negative news that bombarded you all day.

If it bleeds, it leads is the old news headline adage. But now it seems as if every headline bleeds. Every bit of news is treated as a crisis of epic proportions that could threaten your well-being.

When you aren't careful about monitoring your communication intake, anxiety can seep into your soul and accumulate to the point it becomes a toxic waste site within you. Eventually this anxiety can poison you from within.

Loss

Life means loss. Someone once stated that the way you spell grief is *l-o-s-s*. We enter the world with nothing except our bodies. Then we spend the rest of our lives losing everything we have ever accumulated and possessed—including our bodies (1 Timothy 6:7).

You are anxious about losing your job and not having enough money to live on—both now and after retirement. You are nervous about health concerns. Are you a doctor's visit away from a cancer diagnosis? You fear a financial collapse. Are your investments secure? If not, what then? Every major election cycle seems to enlist the economy as a major priority to people. *Are you better off now than you were in the past election cycle?* is a question asked by political candidates.

According to a 2018 Gallup poll,[2] Americans were most concerned about:

1. Healthcare (55 percent)

2. Crime and violence (51 percent)

3. Social Security system (44 percent)

4. Economy (34 percent)

The ultimate loss is your life. Aging. And death. Your body becomes weaker. Eventually, you will die.

The number of potential losses are as many as you can imagine.

And with each thought about another potential loss, anxiety increases.

Loneliness

Experts believe there is an increasing epidemic of loneliness. Even though we've never been so digitally connected, young people especially are grappling with loneliness. Some experts have suggested that the side effects are as bad as smoking 15 cigarettes per day.[3]

People's increasing isolation from others exacerbates anxiety.

The problem of loneliness isn't all that recent. According to Robert Putnam, in his landmark work *Bowling Alone,* Americans began living in increasing loneliness in the 1990s. Social capital has decreased. People have come to live more and more apart from others. Even in places where socializing normally takes place, like bowling alleys, people have started bowling alone. Without a team, all alone.

Some sociologists have termed this dilemma as *kinlessness.* Kinfolk are no longer a part of many people's lives.

And this problem is worsening. The divorce rate has not abated. People are continuing to move all over the country, separating themselves from family. They don't know their neighbors. Disposable hours are spent in front of a screen, not face to face with a real human.

Young adults are delaying marriage. Some are choosing never to have children, who could later care for them when they are less able to care for themselves. Others want to have one, maybe two children at the most. Many are choosing not to marry at all.

In our increasingly disconnected society, questions abound. How can Social Security be secure if there won't be enough workers to pay into it in the decades to come? Who will care for the seniors of the future when they are in their 80s and 90s? Or those who become disabled or infirmed? Can immigrants help fill this void? If so, what kind of America are we facing in the future? Will it even come close to resembling the America we've known and loved?

Britain is so concerned about this problem that the government has formed a new cabinet position called the Minister of Loneliness.[4] Their leaders see the impending isolation tsunami crashing on their culture.

Many in America see the same problem looming on the horizon, which will surely become a major source of anxiety.

Moreover, social scientists see a connection between anxiety and the Internet.[5] Through social media, people can be connected with others all over the globe. From work associates to childhood friends, we can connect with the click of a button. Never has communication been so simple.

But as more and more people spend countless hours in front of a screen, they are becoming increasingly *less* connected. Studies show that more and more Americans feel lonely and isolated. There is little face-to-face time. Touching. Laughter. Hugging. Relationships have grown more superficial. Fewer people are talking with others about the deep matters of the heart.

Apps are being designed to help mend lonely hearts. The Peanut app helps to connect women who feel stuck in their homes or disenfranchised. It enables women to interact face to face and generates around 200,000 swipes per day.

Talkspace offers options to those who can't afford traditional in-person therapy. Through a payment plan, people can connect with a licensed therapist. Patients can reach out 24/7, as opposed to having to set appointments. One of the appeals is that people who are struggling with high levels of loneliness don't have to wait until the next appointment to get help. But all the interaction is limited to a screen.

Here is the problem: You can't read social and facial cues very well on a screen. It's hard to figure out what another person is feeling via a screen. Did you know that empathy shrivels with repeated digital usage?[6] Social intelligence diminishes as well via constant social media usage. Nonverbal communication is very difficult.

Social media sites emphasize the quantity of people you have as followers, not the quality. The average Facebook user has 338 friends.[7] But how can you be deeply involved with that many people? It's impossible.

In fact, some studies suggest that the more friends you have on social media, the more anxious you feel. You can't communicate deeply with all or even most of them. It's impossible.

Think about those times when you are at a restaurant with friends. It's not possible to engage with everyone at the same level. Another problem is that some people are glancing at their smartphone or texting, which diminishes the social interaction. People aren't giving their full attention to others for an extended period of time. They aren't listening carefully.

A recent study showed Americans check their smartphones 80 times per day.[8] With younger people, it's likely more often than that. Ironically, people scroll down on their phones to find out what others are doing while ignoring their most important relationships in their immediate presence.

The Internet has increased our ability to work remotely. But that also means less interaction with colleagues. When you work directly with others, comradery and friendship increases. Working remotely decreases the possibility of deep friendships.

Which, in turn, can exacerbate anxiety.

Loneliness is an especially growing problem among men. The American culture teaches rugged individualism—that masculinity is a lone-wolf experience. Men aren't supposed to be close to each other. Or cry. Therefore, they are expected to face a competitive, wolf-eat-wolf culture alone.

Which means they are also expected to hide their anxiety. But undeniably, it's there!

> In the Bible, the church is called
> the body of Christ. We're meant
> to interact face to face.

As the loneliness grows, Christians must ask this question: How do we understand all the "one another" commands in the Bible (love, encourage, pray for, build up, carry burdens, etc.)? It's more difficult to do "one another" ministry with anyone while looking at a screen. And please note that these "one another" exhortations are imperatives, not suggestions from God's Word.

The Lord knows the importance of people being together. Of your life being intertwined with other lives. Remember, in the Bible, the church is called the body of Christ. We're meant to interact face to face.

Loneliness is a serious source of anxiety, and it's only getting worse.

Nature's Disasters

Hardly a week passes by without news of another earthquake, hurricane, flood, forest fire, or tornado somewhere in the world. And social media incessantly feeds pictures of these devastating events to your mind.

As of this writing, two hurricanes, Florence and Michael, have rampaged through the state of North Carolina. They arrived within several weeks of one another.

People in the eastern part of the state were beginning to see floodwaters recede after Florence's entrance from the Atlantic Ocean. After assessing Florence's damage, they breathed a collective sigh of anguish, trying to figure out how to rebuild their lives. A grueling future awaited them.

Then, within weeks, came Michael—a Category 4 hurricane from the Gulf of Mexico. It not only destroyed towns on the Gulf Coast, it dropped several more inches of rain on the eastern part of North Carolina. The rain set people back even further from where they were after Florence. This second round of flooding was tragic and seemed cruel.

No place is immune to nature's fury. Disasters can happen to any of us at any time. *Is my home next? Will it soon happen to me and my family? My town? When will it happen? Soon? Will I have enough time to prepare? Do I have enough insurance?*

The more you dwell on these kinds of questions while fixating your mind on possible disasters, the more anxiety will grow within you.

Wars and Rumors of Wars

More wars were fought in the twentieth century than in any previous one. The twenty-first century has not given much hope that wars will decrease over the next 100 years.

At the time of this writing, the Syrian Civil War will soon enter its eighth year. Most of the world seems to hate Israel and wants to see the Jewish people pushed into the Mediterranean Sea. Globally, nations continue to rise up against nations.

More countries than ever before are armed with nuclear capabilities. Other nations are close to having them. Several are hostile to the United States. Sabre-rattling among leaders has grown. Threats of attack and retaliation abound between world leaders. "If you cross this line, then we will retaliate with an unimaginable force that will wipe you from the face of the earth."

On January 13, 2018, someone in Hawaii detected an incoming missile from North Korea. He pushed the warning button, sending out an alert signal. Panic quickly ensued all over Hawaii—a terror that soon engulfed the West Coast of the United States as well. For 38 minutes, many people suffered a deep, foreboding state of anxiety, thinking their worst fears were about to be realized. They were convinced that a nuclear war had begun between the United States and North Korea.

The alert was soon determined to be a false alarm. There was a collective sigh of relief from millions of people. But for 38 minutes, many were convinced a nuclear Armageddon had commenced. Even after the matter was reported as a false alarm, people began to wonder if this was a warning for what is to come.

For the moment, the strength of the jihadist militant group ISIS has dissipated. They clearly are not as strong as they were. But many have wondered if the present victory is only temporary, and ISIS might eventually return to full strength to pursue its aggressive ideology.

My wife Marilynn and I recently journeyed to Lebanon, desiring especially to visit Syrian refugee camps. We wanted to see how we could help address the extraordinary human needs there.

Astonishingly, when members of our congregation learned of our trip, they became anxious for us. They encouraged us not to go, convinced that we were placing ourselves in harm's way. They warned us of the possibility of being either kidnapped or killed by ISIS soldiers. They were certain our trip was a risky endeavor we should not undertake.

Marilynn and I chose not to let our hearts be troubled. We would not allow these anxious thoughts to enter our minds. We knew that God had called us to go to Lebanon. We were convinced that the safest place to be is in God's will. And where God guides, he always provides for our every need.

When Marilynn and I arrived in Lebanon, we were curious whether the people there felt anxious about ISIS. We asked our friends there if they were worried about this group. Interestingly, they merely shrugged their shoulders, even chuckling a bit.

Yes, they lived daily with the threat of ISIS, but were unconcerned. When they received Jesus as their Lord and Savior, they had placed their lives in God's hands and trusted themselves to his care. They believed the Lord who oversaw the angel armies in heaven would protect them.

Marilynn and I were struck by the obvious irony: Americans were anxious about ISIS even though they lived thousands of miles away from the epicenter of Mideast terror. Yet those Christians who lived next door to ISIS lived anxiety-free. We couldn't help but ask, "Hmmm, what is wrong with this picture?"

Even so, terrorist attacks *do* still happen around the globe. They *do* continue. They *are* a threat.

A 2015 Gallup poll said that 51 percent of Americans were more anxious about becoming a victim of terrorism.[9] Who can stop lone-wolf attacks? How can we stop someone who has set his heart on blowing himself up to destroy others?

Our enemy, Satan, wants you to focus your mind on wars and rumors of wars. Threats and potential future threats. Anything that will make anxious thoughts grow in your mind. He realizes that when anxiety increases, so does unbelief. He knows that when faith is lacking, you're more likely to doubt God. So, he keeps pounding your mind with anxious thoughts.

That is the enemy's plan—his scheme, his strategy. It's worked from the beginning, and there is no reason for him to stop.

Are you aware of the enemy's plans?

Negative Medical Diagnoses

A 2018 Gallup poll addressing what Americans worry about indicated that 55 percent of Americans were most anxious about the availability of healthcare. Another 44 percent were worried about the solvency of the Social Security system.[10]

The cost of healthcare *is* rising. There seems to be nothing in the near future that will help abate costs. Each election cycle brings more and more promises from politicians to address the problem, but nothing ever seems to get done. Any hope that people have about healthcare issues being addressed is becoming replaced by anxiety that nothing will ever get done.

And each medical visit generates a foreboding cloud of anxiety over what a doctor may discover. A simple chest X-ray, or blood work, or a probe around the neck or back may cause worry. *Might I get a phone call in a few days dealing a body blow to all my life plans? And will I be able to afford what I may be facing? What about my family? I don't want to be a burden to them.*

All of those concerns and questions reveal the underlying problem: anxiety about death. Many want to deny the reality that everyone dies. The statistics don't lie: One out of one *does* die.

Death is inescapable and inevitable, no matter how healthy you are right now. It's a reality we all face. And death reminds us all that we are not really in control of anything—including our health.

Anxiety can result from your desire to control your life. But you can't. Death reminds you of this fact.

And that's what Satan wants your mind to focus on.

Failure

We live in a society that says your worth is found in your work. In a performance-driven world, what you do determines who you are. Your identity is bound up in your personal success.

Your value rests in contributing to a productive economy. Old foundations for meaning—such as parenthood, civic involvement, and church membership—have become less important in a culture that only cares about your ability to produce. The emphasis on benefiting social order has been replaced with efficiency. Your value comes from being a part of whatever society says is the greater good.

That's why people are afraid to fail. They hesitate to try something new, creative, or innovative. *I cannot fail; I will have no value if I do.*

This fear of failure puts us in the dark prison of anxiety.

And the enemy loves it when our thoughts are fixed there.

Rejection

Rejection is acid rain on the soul. It corrodes a sense of worth like nothing else. It too moves people toward isolation and a lack of human interaction. *If I was hurt once, I can be hurt again.*

Therefore, the safest way to avoid rejection is to have no close, meaningful relationships.

People who have experienced rejection tend to hold on to bitterness. They remain angry with those who hurt them. They can't or won't let go of the pain. They yearn for vengeance and vindication. When it doesn't come, they become bitter toward God. They wonder if he is just and fair. Sometimes they think he may be punishing them for some wrongdoing.

The anxiety that comes with rejection usually ends up increasing people's isolation. They are certain another rejection will occur. So they never risk loving again.

These negative, fear-filled thoughts rummage constantly through their minds.

And the devil cackles with delight, knowing where this type of thinking will lead: chronic anxiety.

Not Having Enough of _____

Studies have identified a major negative emotion produced by social media. Can you guess what it is? Envy.

Why is this the case?

People rarely post statements or pictures that are negative about themselves. They almost always show their smiles, the fun they are having, the breathtaking destination they are visiting, and all the smiling friends surrounding them.

On the outside, everyone appears perfect. On the inside, they are not.

But when you look at other people's social media news and pictures, you assume that everything must be going great for them. *Why isn't life working out like that for me? Why am I struggling?*

So you feel envy. Maybe you are angry with God that you aren't experiencing what others are.

You start to compare your insides with someone else's outsides. How dangerous! Your mind focuses on what you don't have.

The enemy loves it when you do this.

When you compare yourself with others, only two things can happen, and both of them are negative. First, you will feel envy or jealousy because you don't have what others have. Or you will feel pride because you have more than what others have.

Both envy and pride are deadly to your soul—both are rooted in the need to be competitive and win. You forget that envy and pride were what caused the enemy to become God's enemy.

The devil didn't like Jesus's position on the throne of heaven. He led a rebellion to overthrow Jesus so he could have this place of authority for himself.

The enemy's envy and pride caused his eventual expulsion from heaven. Because he can't have heaven's throne, he now wants the throne in your mind. That's why he keeps planting anxious thoughts within you—thoughts suggesting you need _____ to be happy.

In my hometown of Charlotte, North Carolina, there is a monthly magazine that highlights stories of interest for the affluent. One issue had this title on its front cover: "Closet Envy."[11]

No kidding.

Admittedly, when I first saw the issue, I was taken aback. A feature article about closet envy? In a city where homelessness is a prodigious problem, there is a magazine depicting closet envy as a matter that needs to be examined?

The story gave a glimpse inside the closets of three Charlotte women to examine their "sartorial splendor—to show that it's possible for one of the most overlooked rooms of the home to also be one of the most glamorous."[12]

When the square footage of their closets was given, I realized that they were bigger than some rooms in many other people's homes. They had to be that large to contain all those shoes, dresses, shirts, and clothes.

Are we in America now creating closet envy?

This is yet another example of how we tend to find our identity by comparing ourselves with others. *My closet is bigger than yours. I have more clothes and shoes than you do.*

Ultimately, the message is this: I am better than you are. I'm more successful. I have more value.

If only I had _____. You fill in the blank. Whatever it is you long for, it's a snare for you to compare yourself to others.

The problem is that when you play this game, you will never have enough. There will always be someone bigger, stronger, faster, richer, more famous, more gifted, and more qualified than you.

Contentment is impossible, a mere illusion. You can never know the meaning of this Bible verse: "Godliness with contentment is great gain" (1 Timothy 6:6).

When you are discontent, the evil one is very pleased. He has you where he wants you.

He has your mind focused on the superficial, not the significant. On the transitory, not the eternal.

And you will become increasingly anxious.

Political Divisions

America has never been more divided than it is today. Spontaneous outrage increases by the day. It's seen everywhere—particularly when it comes to identity politics. Those who identify as part of a group—whether by gender, race, or some other distinctive—detest certain other groups. They do everything they can to make their perceived opponents look bad. Gotcha politics abounds.

Conservatives and liberals alike are hounded by angry people, even driven out of public restaurants by protesters who find their politics offensive. Explosive devices are sent through the mail. The senders are conservatives and progressives alike. One politician was even shot by an angry person because of his political affiliation and beliefs.

Party politics have stymied leaders from making needed decisions to address the country's problems. Mistrust is everywhere. Unity is elusive. Collaboration seems impossible.

Few want to heed the warning that a nation divided against itself cannot stand.

How many people realize that the devil is a divider? He wants to separate us from one another. To break us down into smaller groups. He wants hate, not love, to rule our lives.

As hatred and division increase, anxiety grows in our minds.

And the enemy rejoices—because he knows that if he can divide people, he can conquer them.

Tomorrow

All of us worry about tomorrow—about what *might* happen to us.

But no one knows what tomorrow may bring. Crises loom everywhere. New ones seem to pop up daily. When and where will the next shoe drop? What could happen next? Will tomorrow be worse than today?

As those who follow Jesus, we need to turn to our Lord and ask him how we should look at tomorrow. When we do, we will find that he gives us a clear admonition: Do *not* to worry about tomorrow (Matthew 6:34). He said that tomorrow presents enough problems of its own. He adjured us to focus on today.

> **Whatever God calls you to go through, he will give you the grace you need to deal with it.**

This day, today, is the day that the Lord has made. Let us rejoice and be glad in it (Psalm 118:24).

And as you enjoy today to the full, believe that the Lord will give you enough grace to face your circumstances. Whatever God calls you to go through, he will give you the grace you need to deal with it.

Jesus said that in this world you will have tribulation (John 16:33). We all face difficulties.

Consider the fact that rain brings both blessings and floods—to the righteous and unrighteous alike (Matthew 5:45). Your job is to fix your thoughts on the Rainmaker, the one who controls all the rain, Jesus your Lord. You are to focus on the reminder that though there are tribulations in this world, you are to rejoice. Be glad. Enjoy life. Jesus said, "Take heart; I have overcome the world" (John 16:33).

Final Thoughts

Anxiety is a real problem. It's not going away any time soon.

Can you do anything about your worries? Is there hope?

The answer is an overwhelming shout of yes!

Though the battle in your mind seems overwhelming, it can be won. Though anxiety rages and wants to control your life, you don't have to succumb to it. Why?

Because we can "have the mind of Christ" (1 Corinthians 2:16). Allow

Jesus to control your thought life. You can think as Jesus thought and live as he lived. Jesus can help you to spot lies and give you the power to take every thought captive.

Victory can be yours. You *can* win. There *is* a remedy for anxiety.

Here is the key: You must use God's weapons. You can't use a water pistol to fight a rattlesnake. You must use spiritual weapons to defeat a spiritual foe.

Where should you begin?

You must start with the weapon of faith. You must replace all anxiety with total faith in God. Surrender. Trust. Belief. In any and all areas of your life and mind.

There is no part of your mind that can be left vulnerable to the enemy. You cannot allow him to possess one thought or to plant worry in your mind.

Thoughts filled with faith will conquer anxiety. Not a little faith, but great faith. Not a dab of faith, but a dominant faith.

A great faith in God is where the cure for anxiety begins.

Let's counter anxiety with faith.

In the rest of this book, we'll learn how to do that.

PART 2:

OVERCOMING ANXIETY

CHAPTER 3

FOCUS ON FAITH

The spiritual enemy of your soul doesn't want you to live a life filled with joy and peace. He would prefer that your heart be filled with anxiety. He wants you to be weighed down with the cares of this world and paralyzed by the pain of all your burdens.

Is your heart weighed down with worry? Has hope evaporated? Is anxiety the most dominant emotion you are experiencing now?

If you find yourself answering yes to these questions, let me tell you about the importance of focusing your faith on Jesus. This is what has helped countless numbers of people through the ages overcome the problem of worry.

Focusing on faith in Jesus will free you from all anxiety.

It Begins with Faith

Victory over anxiety begins with faith. What you believe influences how you feel. And faith is God's antidote to anxiety.

In Hebrews 11 is a list of God's heroes—people who accomplished great things for him. Some call this list "God's Hall of Fame of Faith." Many of the works done by these people were miraculous. How did they overcome their difficult circumstances? Not with worry, but through faith. Repeatedly, each verse says so.

When Jesus's followers expressed anxiety, he chided them for having "little faith" (Luke 12:28). He asked them why they were afraid, and then lovingly lectured them about the importance of possessing faith (Matthew

8:26). He said this after he calmed a storm, and Jesus's words appear to imply that *the disciples'* faith could have calmed the storm.

When Jesus taught his disciples about worry, he said to them, "If God so clothes the grass of the field…will he not much more clothe you, O you of little faith?" (Matthew 6:30). On another occasion he said that the people who lived in certain cities could not witness his mighty miracles because of their lack of faith (Matthew 13:58).

Conversely, Jesus affirmed two examples of great faith. A Roman centurion believed that if Jesus just said "the word," his servant would be healed (Matthew 8:8). Jesus marveled at his faith, and the servant was healed. And a Syrophoenician woman asked Jesus to heal her little girl. Though Jesus seemed at first to rebuff her request, she persisted. She wouldn't give up. Jesus marveled to others about her great faith, and he healed her daughter (Mark 7:35-40).

Would Jesus call your faith great or little? Be honest—especially as you think about and confront your anxiety.

Hebrews 11:6 clearly states that without faith, it is impossible to please God. Not hard or difficult, but impossible.

The Battle in Your Mind

There is a battle being waged in your mind. In one corner is faith. In the other is anxiety. The corner on which you focus your thoughts will determine which side wins. It's your choice. Your battle. No one else can fight it for you. You alone determine the victory by deciding whether you focus your mind on faith or anxiety. This choice determines the outcome of the battle.

Jesus said to his followers, "Let not your hearts be troubled" (John 14:1). *Let not.* Apparently, Jesus taught that *you* are the one who chooses to allow your heart to be troubled or not. It is your choice.

The battle is in your mind—anxiety versus faith. You alone decide where to focus your thoughts.

But don't miss the second part of Jesus's admonition in John 14:1. After exhorting you not to let your heart be troubled, he clearly stated, "Believe in God. Believe also in me." As you choose to believe in him and the Father, you will receive the needed strength and faith to heal your troubled heart.

You *can* win the battle over anxiety.

> **If you choose to focus your mind on anxiety, faith flees. And if you choose to focus your thoughts on faith, anxiety leaves.**

Jesus urged his followers to be anxious for nothing (Matthew 6:25). *Nothing.* Not one thing should ever worry you. Apparently, Jesus doesn't want you to allow a single worrisome thought to invade your mind.

If you choose to focus your mind on anxiety, faith flees. And if you choose to focus your thoughts on faith, anxiety leaves.

Anxiety and faith are at odds with one another. They are ferocious foes that are totally incompatible.

A healthy mind cannot focus on both. And remember the biblical definition of anxiety: a divided mind.

Victory Through Faith

The Bible makes it clear that anxiety can be overcome. It repeatedly gives one major answer on how to defeat it: by faith. Believe. Trust God. Surrender all to him. Complete, unyielding, unabashed, surrendered faith in your Creator is the answer to anxiety. A trust that rests completely in God's loving arms.

The victory that overcomes the world is *your* faith (1 John 5:4). No matter what your circumstances may be, God oversees them. Everything is under his sovereign, gracious control. You can trust your heavenly Father like a child does his earthly father. No weapon formed against you can prosper (Isaiah 54:17). You are secure in his hands.

When faith is chosen over anxiety, we become "more than conquerors"—*huper-nike*, according to the original Greek text (Romans 8:37). We don't just overcome; we are *more* than overcomers. Through Jesus, we can be super-conquerors over every anxious thought.

When we choose to have faith in every storm, anxiety slinks away in defeat. And peace enters our minds and hearts.

When Life Hurts

Yes, we can experience victory over anxiety even when tragedy strikes. When life hurts. When things aren't going well. When the battle is especially difficult. It's easy to believe we'll know victory when everything is fine. It's harder to trust God when life is falling apart.

But tragic times test—and strengthen—our faith. It's the tests that show whether we really believe or not. Whether we totally trust or not. That's why a teacher gives an exam to the pupils. He wants to see whether the class knows the information.

The Father loves it when you take the test of faith and refuse to give in to despair. That's your way of getting an *A* on God's exam.

Conversely, the enemy is bewildered. He cannot understand how you remain steadfast in belief after he has caused all your circumstances to fall apart. He is stunned that you still love God and trust him in everything.

The enemy hisses in disgust when you give evidence of true faith in your life. He doesn't like it when you thwart his powerful weapon of anxiety. And God smiles with delight when you place your complete trust in him.

Faith believes that God is working through your current problems for an ultimate good. You believe that somehow, in some way, the Father is with you in your difficult situations. You are absolutely convinced of this.

You walk through the dark nights of the soul believing that victory will come. Though you may face a cross, you believe that a resurrection will occur. You live on the tiptoe of expectation. Something good *will* happen. You are certain of it. As a result, hope replaces despair. Joy overwhelms sorrow.

As you walk through the valley of the shadow of death, you still believe that God is present with all his comfort (Psalm 23:4). You are certain that heaven is your home. What can the enemy do to you? He is a defeated foe. Death is not the final word; eternal life is.

You proclaim with Joseph that though others meant to do evil against you, God meant it for good (Genesis 50:20). You know that God is good and his steadfast love endures forever (Psalm 100:5).

You are certain that God is present in your pain. His purposes are being worked out. And even your current suffering is light and momentary in comparison to the eternal glory that awaits you in heaven (2 Corinthians 4:17). You know that nothing can ever separate you from his love (Romans 8:39).

And you are convinced that God's overarching providence will bring eventual victory. It may not happen tomorrow. Or in the near future. But it *will* happen in God's perfect timing. God never answers *no* to your prayer. His apparent rejection is actually a new direction for your life.

You also believe that at the end of history, when Jesus returns, all evil will be overcome. All injustice will be dealt with. Everyone will be held accountable for how they have lived their lives. No one will get away with anything. Everything broken will be mended. All will be used for good. Everything will be restored to its original order (Acts 3:21).

God will win. It's the victory shout of the believer in Jesus.

Therefore, why worry about anything? You choose to believe.

A Test for You

As previously mentioned, teachers give tests in school for one simple reason: They want to know if you know the information. Tests are essential for learning—especially in the area of faith.

Consequently, there is an easy test that you can give yourself to see where your mind is focused. You can quickly discern if you have centered your mind on belief or anxiety.

Get alone. Close the door and window shades. Lower the lights. Be still. Eliminate all noise. Quiet your soul. Turn off your phone, television, and computer. Remove all distractions. Close your eyes. Breathe deeply in and out. Feel your heart rate get slower and slower. Clear your mind of everything. Try as best as you can to place your brain on idle.

Then wait. Wait some more. And maybe even some more. Take at least five minutes in this state of silence, perhaps longer. Then start to identify your thoughts as they enter your brain.

Now ask yourself: What is coming to your mind? Try to acknowledge every single one. Were they thoughts of God's love, peace, and security? Or thoughts of worry, anxiety, and despair?

Now take a pen and a piece of paper and write down as many thoughts as you can remember that entered your mind. Make sure you are specific. Try to remember them all.

What does this list of your thoughts show you? They should expose what your mind has been dwelling on. What you have been thinking over the previous minutes and hours.

Everyone is thinking about something, all day long. Your brain doesn't ever stop thinking about something. It's always in motion, constantly whirring with new thoughts and ideas. And you tend to focus on what's foremost in your life.

You now know where your thought life is focused. You see your mind's priorities. You are able to know if anxiety is consuming your thought life.

Once you know what you've been thinking, you can start to choose a different path. You choose *not* to let your heart be troubled. You choose to believe Jesus and all his promises.

You start to reboot your mind with faith-filled thoughts.

Please Remember This

My wife Marilynn hates it when we are watching television and a gross, violent picture flashes across the screen. It can come unexpectedly in a commercial or as a part of a program. When this happens, she tries to hide her eyes as quickly as possible.

Marilynn calls it *assaulting her senses.*

That's a good image. A fearful, negative, or godless thought from the screen assaults your mind. It attacks your brain. It hurts your heart.

Why does Marilynn hate it when this happens? Once an image gets into your mind, it's very difficult to remove it. Your mind places a spotlight on the garbage that's just entered. You can't *stop* thinking about it, no matter how hard you try.

And what happens next? As you ponder what you've just seen, anxiety rises and suffocates faith.

Always remember to be careful about what you watch. Gross images create thoughts. They are not neutral. And if you place godless garbage in your mind, negative feelings such as anxiety must follow.

You feel what you think. Troublesome thoughts trouble your spirit.

By the way, Marilynn reminds our adult children of this same truth. She repeatedly reminds them: *Garbage in, garbage out.* She especially doesn't want our grandkids to see anything that is evil. If something is true it is true for adults and children alike.

Marilynn is a very wise person.

Freedom from Anxiety

Jesus wants to set you free from anxiety. He came to set the captives free (Luke 4:18), especially those incarcerated in the prison of anxiety. He said if you abide in him, and his truth abides in you, that the truth will set you free (John 8:32).

Don't you want to be free from worry?

> **The closer you come to Jesus, the farther anxiety removes itself from you.**

Faith is the key for Jesus's followers to experience his freedom. Resting in a close, intimate relationship with him assures you that he alone possesses all power and glory. His light drives the deep, dark shadows of anxiety away. The closer you come to Jesus, the farther anxiety removes itself from you. Anxiety's darkness hates to be close to the Light of the world, Jesus (John 8:12).

Look at Jesus's life. He calmed storms. Exorcized the demonic. Healed the sick. Gave sight to the blind. Allowed the lame to walk. The dead were raised to new life. All happened because he believed that he was living in the Father's perfect will. He operated his life in absolute surrender and total faith.

Jesus only did what the Father told him to do (John 6:38). Obedience was the proof of his faith. His only desire was to obey the will of the Father.

And the Father rejoiced in Jesus's perfect faith. The Father's life flowed through him accordingly. And it can through you as well.

Faith in the Father was the source of Jesus's power. And faith grants this same efficacy to Jesus's followers as well.

The same power that raised Jesus from the dead now resides in the mind of Jesus's followers (Romans 8:11). The glory that Jesus had with the Father is the same glory his followers now possess (John 17:22). The one who lives in you, Jesus, is greater than the one who lives in the world—the enemy (1 John 4:4). The Father's perfect love living in you casts out all fear (1 John 4:18). Not some, but *all* fear.

Ponder those promises. Focus your thoughts on these truths. Let them sink deeply inside your mind. Their reality should cause your heart to abound with hope. Let your mind be ignited with an assurance that anxiety is not God's will for you.

And possess the faith of a child. It is an especially potent kind of faith, Jesus said (Mark 10:15).

A childlike faith shows utter dependence on the father. You just know that Daddy will protect you. Provide for you. Oversee and guide you. Give grace to your every moment. In every situation of your life, his loving arms will surround you. Hold you closely and never forsake you.

Jesus wants to set you free from all anxiety.

And faith in him causes fear to flee.

The Definition of Faith

What is faith? There is only one definition in the Bible. It's the assurance of things hoped for, the convictions of things not seen (Hebrews 11:1). Though you can't see all of God's promises, you still believe them. They are true simply because the Father in heaven said so.

You can choose to walk by faith and not by sight (2 Corinthians 5:7). You can choose to trust the one you can't see rather than succumb to the negative circumstances surrounding you.

Your thoughts will run to where you direct them. You either focus on God or the problem.

Faith unleashes God's power to fight all his enemies—especially anxiety. God hates anxiety. It has rotted the minds of too many of his children. He despises what it has done to those whom he loves so dearly.

God wants us to fight anxiety. Get rid of it. See it gone. Forever cast it into the pit of hell.

God wants us to hate anxiety like he does.

Fighting the Battle

There *is* hope for those filled with anxiety. You *can* be set free. You don't have to let your heart be troubled. You do *not* have to live in a chronic state of worry. You can know victory. You can be set free. The enemy of your soul can be defeated.

The battlefield is in your mind. That is where the battle with anxiety is fought. It is a furious fight of faith (1 Timothy 6:12). The enemy relentlessly attacks, but you can win.

Start the fight today.

Don't allow your heart to be troubled anymore. God has not left you hopeless and powerless. There are action steps you can take. You have an arsenal more potent that the enemy's wiles.

The First Step

Here is the first step: Start focusing on your faith. Begin with the undeniable fact that Jesus has won. Because of his resurrection and ascension, he has overcome sin, death, and the devil. The power that lifted up Jesus now lives in you.

And this power in you now overcomes anxiety.

Don't casually breeze through this profound biblical truth. Pause and ponder this astonishing reality. Not just once, but over and over again.

Right now, at this very moment, Jesus sits at the right hand of the Father ruling over everything in the universe. That includes you and all you are presently experiencing, including your anxiety. They are small problems in comparison to God's power that now lives in you.

Jesus yearns to give you victory over your fears and anxieties. He doesn't want them to haunt your heart anymore. And the power that gives you this victory now resides *in* you!

Choose to believe. Focus on your faith.

Believe that God not only exists, but he created all. He created humans. He created you. He had a plan for all creation that was ransacked by disobedience and rebellion. The evil one led the rebellion. He is still trying to recruit followers to keep the rebellion going. Choose to enlist in God's army. Know without any doubt that you are on God's side and he is on yours.

Realize that anxiety was never a part of God's original design. It's a foreign invasion into God's purposes. God wants hearts filled with faith. He doesn't want you to live in anxiety anymore.

It's time for you to win, to have victory over anxiety. To crush its evil head under *your* feet. To declare and see it gone forever. To cast it into the pit of hell where it belongs. Let the devil and his angels live in anxiety about their eternal destination.

But not you. You, as a child of God, can live in peace, hope, and love. With a perfect faith that throttles all the enemy's wiles. The same faith that allowed Jesus to calm storms is the same faith that now lives in you.

Final Thoughts

When the enemy punches your mind with anxiety, you *must* counterpunch with faith.

What does faith look like? And how can you live out this faith?

That's what the rest of this book is about. You'll read about some specific tools, rooted in faith, that can help you win over anxiety. Each one is important; make sure you use them all. Don't remove one from your arsenal.

You will need them all at different points in your war against anxiety. To counterpunch his assaults.

But *always* remember: You *can* defeat anxiety. It is not stronger than the Jesus who lives in you.

That is a promise direct from God's Word to your mind.

CHAPTER 4

PRAY

Many have said that whatever occupies your mind will largely govern what you do. Said another way, you do what you think. Your beliefs cause your behavior.

The enemy fully understands this truth. That's why he attacks your thought life. He knows that your battle against anxiety begins and ends in the mind. You are what you think and what you choose to believe.

That is why Christians are called to take every thought captive (2 Corinthians 10:5). Not even one can be left unattended. That means taking your anxious thoughts captive as well.

Before you permit anxiety to become a squatter in your mind, you must place a *No Trespassing* sign at the door of your mind. It is *your* mind that God has given you, not the enemy's. You are its overseer. The enemy is not welcome, much less allowed to enter.

You must learn how to nip your thoughts in the bud, as my mom used to counsel me. Stop the anxious thoughts before they can ever enter and take root.

Before worry has access, room, and board in your mind, you want to arrest it at the doorway. You want to take authority over it in the mighty name of Jesus. He has authority over this negative feeling.

So spear anxiety aggressively with great vigor. Confront its ugly face and command it to leave. You may even need to become angry with your anxious thoughts. After all, if you leave them unattended, they can destroy you. There is such a thing as righteous anger. Anything that hampers God's will should motivate righteous anger.

And anxiety is *not* from the Lord.

Jesus is Lord; anxiety is not. When it's confronted, it *must* surrender. Take your anxious thoughts prisoner and escort them far away from your thought life forever.

Let's look at a formidable weapon you can use to eradicate worry from your mind.

Using Prayer to Defeat Anxiety

A potent instrument for usurping your anxious thoughts is prayer, especially prayer with faith. It is a powerful weapon given to you by your Father in heaven. You must pray regularly to keep anxiety away from you.

Someone once said that effective prayer is simply healthy thinking informed by God's Word. God's Word is true (John 17:17). Lies must flee before the truth of God's Word. Therefore, when you think God's thoughts, informed by his Word, and then pray God's truth from his Word, emotional health will follow. Worry will depart.

Then you will be transformed by the renewal of your mind (Romans 12:2).

The enemy of your soul does not want you to be emotionally healthy. He knows where you are weak. He plants thoughts in your mind about your weakness and wants you to wallow in worry and be paralyzed with pain.

You must fight the lies of the enemy. When a lie tries to enter your mind, you must spear it. How? By immediately saying a prayer of faith—a prayer that believes God is more powerful than your anxiety.

Jesus Defeated Anxiety

The enemy tried to use anxiety and lies with Jesus. On several occasions, he tried to thwart Jesus from going to the cross.

One such moment occurred when Jesus was on the road to Jerusalem. There, he would face the rejection of the masses and the horrific pain of the cross. When Jesus told his disciples what would soon happen, Peter tried to deter Jesus from going to Jerusalem. But Jesus recognized the enemy's temptations. He understood the voice behind Peter's. He knew the lie the enemy was using in an attempt to gain access to his mind.

"Get behind me, Satan!" he responded (Matthew 16:23).

Jesus knew the enemy's ways of temptation. Satan wanted Jesus to focus on the pain, not the promise. On the problem, not the purpose. The enemy was trying to create anxiety in Jesus's mind to prevent God's will from being done.

And this wasn't the last time the enemy would try to assault Jesus's mind with worry.

That is why Jesus withdrew *often* to pray. For him, prayer wasn't a whim or fancy. Rather, it was a regular discipline, a habit of the heart. Jesus recognized that the strength he needed to overcome the enemy's attacks would come through prayer.

For Jesus, prayer was a priority. A passion. A privilege.

Jesus knew that prayer was God's power source to defeat the enemy. Jesus prayed relentlessly because he knew the enemy would pursue him relentlessly. He knew that other attacks were sure to come.

And they did. After Jesus refused to give in to Peter's warnings, he encountered the enemy again.

When Jesus entered the garden of Gethsemane, he knew that on the next day he would face the gruesome agony of the cross. He went away alone to pray.

The enemy began assaulting Jesus's mind, forcing this question to the surface: *Might there be a way to bypass the cross and still accomplish the Father's will?*

How did Jesus respond to this devious deception? He prayed. He sought the Father's will. He offered up petitions "with loud cries and tears" (Hebrews 5:7). He recognized what the enemy was trying to do—prevent him from going to the cross.

Agonizingly, for an hour, the battle raged in Jesus's mind. Drops of blood poured from his forehead. This was medical evidence of extreme stress. Worry. Anxiety.

Jesus prayed even more fervently. As he did so, he wondered if there was another way.

Finally, Jesus knew what he needed to do. He prayed the kind of prayer that always defeats anxiety—the kind that brings perfect peace whenever it is prayed.

How did Jesus pray? He surrendered *everything* to his Father. He planted the white flag of surrender over every inch of his life. He gave up his right to anything. He relinquished complete control of his life and destiny. He placed himself in the Father's hands and refused to worry. He cast aside all anxiety.

Jesus prayed these simple words: "Not my will, but yours, be done" (Luke 22:42). Nothing more, nothing else.

Game, set, and match. Triumph. Victory over the devil was accomplished. You can picture the enemy slithering away in humiliation. Throttled. Stifled. Defeated. All was now in the Father's hands. The cross was the Father's will. Therefore, it was the Son's will. He prayed *and* obeyed.

For Jesus, peace now replaced anxiety. He would face the cross knowing his life was in his Father's hands. God's will would be done. All would be worked for good.

Jesus prayed. Obeyed. Surrendered. The result? Anxiety fled, and the enemy was defeated.

Jesus's Disciples Witnessed His Prayer Life

Jesus's disciples were observant. Over their years, they had connected his prayer life to his power. They concluded that the reason he could heal the sick, cast out demons, and withstand the withering threats of his enemies was because of his life of prayer.

That is why the disciples asked him to teach them how to pray.

The disciples were smart. They wanted Jesus's power and his peace of mind.

If you want to defeat anxiety, you need to practice prayer like Jesus did. You must pray like Jesus prayed. He does not want you to live in anxiety, but to possess the peace that surpasses all understanding (see Philippians 4:7).

More specifically, you must learn how to pray the prayer of surrender. The enemy hates it when you do.

How do you pray this prayer? As Jesus did in the garden of Gethsemane. You surrender *everything* to the Father's will. *All* your concerns. You refuse to cling to even one. All your problems are in God's hands. It's *his* deal.

It's *his* world. It's *his* job to run his world and your life as *he* sees fit. It's *his* responsibility to take care of it all.

Every. Single. Thing.

It's a prayer that always works to defeat the enemy.

Jesus Is Praying for You

What is prayer? It's simple communication with your closest friend and ally in all the universe, Jesus. It's opening your mind to him and sharing your deepest thoughts. It's knowing that he is praying incessantly for you and all that you are going through (Romans 8:34).

How would your life be different if you could overhear Jesus praying for you? Imagine him on his knees interceding to the Father for you right now. He is praying regularly on your behalf. They are prayers filled with words of care and compassion. Offerings for your future, ones filled with hope.

If you truly believed that Jesus was praying fervently for you right now, how much of your anxiety would flee? Would it melt before the passionate pleas you make to your Lord?

Pray believing that Jesus is praying for you.

He is.

Pray God's Promises

Now empty your anxious mind and fill it with God's promises from his Word. There are thousands of them. Fight the enemy by filling your mind with those promises. Like a child, trust what the Father has told you in his Word. It's *his* Word. Therefore, it must be true (John 17:17).

> **Your anxieties will become increasingly smaller as you place them next to God's promises.**

Memorize God's promises. To memorize something simply means to put it in your mind so that it's always available to immediately recall it when needed.

God is a good father. He is the one who spoke these promises. And good fathers don't lie.

Confront your problems with God's promises. Think about each anxiety. Speak God's Word to it in prayer. If you have multiple anxieties, list all of them. Then write out a promise from God's Word next to each one. You'll find that you can start memorizing God's promises as you write them down. You will also notice that your anxieties will become increasingly smaller as you place them next to God's promises.

Grab your anxiety by the throat. Pray a promise from God's Word in response to it.

God does not want you to medicate the problem. Or deny it ever happened. Or minimize how important it really is. Or bury it deep within your mind. Or excuse its importance. Or beat yourself up that it even happened. Or find your identity in it.

When the enemy invades your mind with thoughts of worry, you are to seize these thoughts with promises from God's Word and pray the problems into oblivion. Never give up (Luke 18:1). Pray with fervor (James 5:16). And without ceasing (1 Thessalonians 5:17).

Pray your anxiety away. Say, "I choose to believe God's promise, not the problem." You are to pummel into submission every worry with God's truth from his Word. Force it into a humiliating surrender. Find the promises that address your anxieties. Memorize them. Place them on the tip of your tongue.

To win the victory over anxiety, you *must* take every anxious thought captive. Every. Single. One. Exercise the power of prayer by praying God's promises—all day long.

The enemy never takes a break. You can't either.

Praying for Anything

"Do not be anxious about anything," Paul said (Philippians 4:6). Anything! That means absolutely nothing should cause you anxiety.

No matter how small or large your worries may be, pray them. No matter how significant or insignificant they may seem, pray them.

Any and all worry-filled thoughts must be taken captive with powerful, fervent, faith-filled prayers. You cannot leave a single one unaddressed. Like a baby snake, if left alone, it can quickly grow and become a larger problem. Cut off its head now, even if it seems small.

Realize that *all* your anxieties are of concern to God. *All* anxieties must be brought to the throne of Jesus. Place them *all* at his feet. Take them *all* off your shoulders and place them on his. Let him carry *all* of them (Matthew 11:28-30).

He cares about every single one of your anxious thoughts. Therefore, carry every one of them to him in prayer.

Don't let a single worry remain in your life.

A Helpful Tip

Visualize a package filled with your worries. You have given them to Jesus. Now imagine him walking away, carrying the package. See him dump them into the depths of the ocean. They sink to the bottom. Invisible from your sight. Gone forever.

That's how Jesus wants you to treat your worries.

In Philippians 4:6, some translations use the word *careful* instead of *anxiety*. Care-full. Think about the meaning of that word. Anxiety is full of cares. To the brim. Spilling over. Overflowing. Sloshing toxicity into your mind.

Now read this verse again and substitute the words *care-full* for *anxiety*. Jesus's followers are to be care-full for nothing. You are not to let your mind be filled with the cares of this world. Not a single worry should be allowed to enter your mind.

That's why it's important for you to have the presence of mind to seek the presence of God. Fill your mind with faith. Trust him. When you pray and trust God's promises, your mind is so full of faith that there is no room for an anxious thought. A *No Vacancy* sign is brightly flashing at your mind's door, alerting all potential anxious tenants that there is no room for them. "Sorry, find another mind to attack," you say to the enemy. "Mine is no longer available."

Jesus knows how much peace you often forfeit because you don't take everything to him in prayer. He understands what needless pain you bear because you don't take all your anxieties to him.

No matter what your worry may be, pray regularly to God. Do not fall prey to worry. Fall to your knees and let God carry all your burdens.

Pray with Thanksgiving

In Philippians 4:6, Paul added an important two-word description of how to pray in faith so that you can conquer worry: "with thanksgiving." A heart of thanks should guide all your prayers.

A simple prayer that eliminates worry is, "Thank you, Lord." Easy. Concise. Poignant. And very potent.

> **Worry cannot share space in your mind when gratitude is present.**

Gratitude is an underutilized weapon for defeating worry. It causes you to pause and think about all the good you have. It makes you focus on the positives surrounding you. Your cup is not only half full, but it also has more blessings than you realized. You are compelled not to forget all your benefits (see Psalm 103:1).

Worry cannot share space in your mind when gratitude is present. If you try to focus on both, you are doubled-minded—the very definition of *anxiety* in the Greek text. Having a divided mind is exhausting. Draining. Depleting. It causes you to be unstable in all you do (James 1:8).

It's impossible to worry and be thankful at the same time. One will eventually overwhelm the other and choke away its life. Fill your mind with thanksgiving.

When you are thankful, and you make a habit of counting all your blessings, you become more empathetic. More gracious. Kinder. More forgiving. More loving. More peaceful.

You see life through the prism of positives, not negatives. Your hope increases. You are convinced there is reason to get up in the morning. A blessed future awaits you. People want to be around you more. Your positive attitude infects others. You sleep better. Bosses at work notice an attitude change that is often rewarded with good work relations—or possibly a raise or a better position.

Consequently, instead of focusing on what you don't have, pray with gratitude. Dwell on what you *do* have. Don't say, "If only I had _____, then I'd be happy." To the contrary! Rather, be happy for all you do have.

"Thank you, Jesus, for all you have given me" should be the constant prayer spoken in your mind—all through your day.

An Example to Follow

I have a friend who continually struggled with anxiety. Daily it besieged every corner of his mind. He was tired all the time. People didn't enjoy being around him. His negativity drained them of their emotional strength. He became increasingly isolated. Hopelessness haunted his heart. He even thought about giving up on life altogether.

Eventually my friend decided to fight back. He realized life still had meaning for him. He wanted to live life to the full, which Jesus promised he can help us do (John 10:10).

My friend entered the fray. He counterpunched the enemy's assaults. He challenged the way he was thinking. He made a decision that altered his life forever.

What did he do? He decided to keep a gratitude journal. Every day he disciplined himself to list the things he was grateful for, and then he lifted up prayers of thanksgiving for what was on his list.

He confessed that at first, this was a laborious exercise. Little progress was made. His mind had been so trained to focus on the negative that he didn't know how to be grateful, much less say prayers of thanksgiving. He would stare at his journal, able to list only a few items.

But he persisted. He refused to give up. He saw all the Bible's commands to be thankful, and he knew God gave those commands for a reason.

For example, my friend read that he was to enter God's presence with thanksgiving and praise (Psalm 100:4). To pray with thanksgiving (Philippians 4:6). To give thanks in all things (1 Thessalonians 5:18).

My friend became increasingly convinced about the power of prayers filled with thanksgiving. He knew that he had to keep trying. With even greater fervor, he disciplined his thought life to focus on gratitude. He forced himself to remember all of God's benefits.

Astonishingly, the more he did so, the longer his list grew. He started discovering all kinds of things to be thankful for. Simple things like air, laughter, hugs, heartbeats, hair, butterflies, dimples, grass, trees, touch, eyesight, hearing, fingernails and toenails, texts, phone calls, coffee, tea, water, the moon, rainbows, a sleeping baby, doctors and nurses, counselors, stars, the sun, and sunshine were added to his list.

The more my friend thought about all the benefits that he enjoyed, the more fun the experiment became. He couldn't wait each morning to continue his gratitude list. To count his blessings.

Days passed by. The gratitude list grew from dozens…to hundreds…to thousands of items. And he prayed about each one. "Thank you, Lord, for butterflies. For bees. For cardinals. For favorite sports teams. Even when they lose! When I don't get my way. When I'm disappointed."

Guess what else happened? With each new notation in his journal and an accompanying prayer of thanksgiving, anxiety began to abate. Lessen. Shrivel. Evaporate.

Like an enemy army that had set up camp in his mind, anxiety began to break camp and retreat—disgraced in defeat. Humbled before his newfound power.

My friend had overwhelmed his worries with prayers of thanksgiving.

After several months of practicing this spiritual discipline, my friend tells me that negative worries can't be found. They have been flushed from his mind and replaced with an attitude of gratitude. Joy has returned and resides with its best friend, peace.

My friend continues to be excited about getting up each morning and enjoying his time of gratitude in prayer. It sets the stage for a day filled with joy and peace.

In Christian parlance, my friend counted his blessings. Literally. Daily. Repeatedly. He won't let a morning go by without praying with thanksgiving. He knows if he doesn't pray, anxiety could easily return with a vengeance. Like an alcoholic who falls off the wagon, he knows the price his mind will pay if he slips into anxiety again.

When anxiety bombards your mind, pray your blessings. Write them down. Keep a journal. Focus your mind on all you *do* have, not what you *don't* have. Do it every day. Don't miss a day, or you will pay a price.

Guess what will happen? Your mind will become connected to the mind of Jesus, your best friend. God's peace will guard your mind in Jesus, your Lord, who controls everything.

The word "guard" in Philippians 4:7 is a military term. It means "a citadel, fortress." It's a guardian for peace in a city. It's a place that protects, oversees, and provides. It feeds needs. It is designed to take care of all the needs of the people within its walls.

Praying with thanksgiving places strong, high, impenetrable walls of protection around your mind. Anxious attacks cannot scale these walls. Therefore, you will experience peace within the citadel in your mind. As we learned earlier, your mind cannot be occupied with anxiety and thanksgiving at the same time.

The potency of prayers of thanksgiving goes far beyond any human understanding. It's impossible to explain. But we know that such prayers really do work.

Final Thoughts

Learn from Jesus. Counterpunch your anxieties with prayer. Make sure your prayers are filled with faith. Say them with thanksgiving as well. Do so every moment, every day. Be thankful for all your many benefits. Count them, speak them, make a list, pray them.

As you do so, your anxieties will dissipate. Become weaker. Feel less threatening. Diminish in your mind…until they no longer control you.

You truly can be more than a conqueror through Jesus (Romans 8:37). Remember—Jesus, who is in you, is greater than the enemy, who constantly attacks your mind with anxiety (1 John 4:4).

Through prayers of thanksgiving, your heart will be troubled no more. God's peace will protect you. Surrender all to Jesus and put your life totally in the hands of your Creator. He loves you, cares for you, and wants to carry your burdens.

God has a future and a hope planned for you. He has a purpose for you because he is good. He's your eternal Daddy. He loves you so much.

It's God's job to rule this world. And your life. Submit all to him through prayer. Surrender yourself and yield to him.

The walls of worry will come tumbling down. And God's peace, which surpasses all understanding, will guard your mind in Christ Jesus from all future anxiety attacks.

CHAPTER 5

FAST

One day while carrying out their ministry, Jesus's disciples encountered a demonic spirit that they could not overcome. Even though Jesus had given them authority over all demonic agencies, they could not cast out this spirit (Mark 9:18). This one was doggedly stubborn. Immovable. It refused to respond to their repeated commands to leave a young boy.

Frustrated, they gave up. Walked away. Heads bowed in defeat.

There was only one thing left to do. They approached Jesus to ask for his help. Surely he knew how to overcome this problem. He would give them a new insight or correct what they were doing wrong.

Jesus assessed the situation. He immediately rebuked the unclean spirit. He spoke forcefully to it: "You mute and deaf spirit, I command you, come out of him and never enter him again" (verse 25). The evil spirit cried out and convulsed the boy terribly. But it left, never to return. The demon fled before Jesus's authority.

At first, the boy lay lifeless, like a corpse. Strangely still. Most of the observers concluded that he was dead. Gone. No hope. Victory for the demonic world.

But Jesus took him by the hand and lifted him up. New life pulsated through his body. The boy arose, healthy and well. He was delivered from the demonic assault and healed.

An incredulous gasp surely consumed the crowd. They had just witnessed the impossible. Hope began to confront their own despair.

The boy moved toward his father. Can you imagine their joy and excitement? Thought dead, the boy was now alive. Well. Whole. Completely restored.

Father and son now entered their house together. A new life would begin for them both. A new home had been created. A vibrant hope had entered their hearts.

But the disciples were confused. They didn't fully understand what had just happened. They thought that they had been given authority over the demonic world. Yet here, in this situation, it seemed the demonic world had authority over them. They had suffered a humiliating setback.

Perplexed, the disciples asked Jesus privately, "Why could we not cast it out?" (verse 28).

Jesus said to them, "This kind [of demon] does not go out except by prayer and fasting" (Matthew 17:21 NASB).

Some problems can be addressed and overcome by prayer alone. There is great power in prayers filled with faith. Fervent prayer does avail much. Jesus's followers are to pray with persistence and never give up. The disciples knew that prayer was the source of all Jesus's power—especially over the enemy's wiles. In the previous chapter, we discovered the power of the prayer of faith for Jesus's followers.

But there appears to be a certain kind of enemy stronghold that even prayers of faith cannot scale. Apparently there are certain powers from the devil, rooted deeply in the mind, that cannot be thwarted by prayers of faith alone.

Another essential ingredient is needed to overcome the problem.

What is that extra power boost we need from the Holy Spirit? We have the answer from Jesus's own lips: There needs to be praying *and* fasting. For certain demonic activity, only praying and fasting together form the potent one-two punch that exorcizes destructive spiritual powers and principalities from your mind.

What Is Fasting?

Fasting is a spiritual discipline that is mentioned throughout the Bible. God's most fervent followers practiced this discipline, most often in times of great need. It's frequently accompanied by weeping and repentance.

For example, when Ezra returned from the Babylonian exile to implement right worship and obedience among the Jews, he discovered that many of them had intermarried with unbelieving foreigners. As a result, these Jews had adopted the pagan practices of their foreigner spouses. Syncretism replaced the worship of the one true God.

This prompted Ezra to start praying and fasting. He interceded for God's people to repent. The people soon did so.

Jesus on Fasting

Jesus expected his followers to fast. As with prayer, Jesus said, "When you fast…," not *if* you fast (Matthew 6:16). Jesus assumed that his disciples would fast regularly—that his followers would use the power of prayer *and* fasting.

When you fast, you are choosing to deny yourself something that normally is important. You are praying in faith to God, "I'm depending totally on you, O Lord, my Creator. Nothing in your creation controls me. Only you do. And as I draw closer to you through this fast, I am certain that you will draw closer to me (James 4:8). I want to see your power meet my life's hopes, hurts, and hang-ups. Only you can meet my needs. During this fast, give me your supernatural strength and power. I want to experience you, Lord, in a new, fresh way."

> The purpose of fasting is to move you into a deeper dependence upon your Creator rather than the creation.

That is how prayer and fasting are inextricably connected.

Again, the purpose of fasting is to move you into a deeper dependence upon your Creator, rather than the creation, for all your needs. Fasting helps make your relationship with Jesus more intimate. It pushes you toward a deeper, more meaningful prayer life. Prayers of faith have more power.

And when there is a strikingly stubborn problem in your life, like chronic anxiety, a fast may be what God wants you to use to give you victory.

Many people have shared how, during a fast, they feel Jesus's presence like never before. They tell of how they experienced anew the full sufficiency of Jesus. They came to realize that he is their everything, their all in all. Their hope. Their life. Their meaning. Their purpose.

Remember, Jesus promised that he is with you always (Matthew 28:20). He will never forsake you (Hebrews 13:5). His very presence can melt your mountains. In fact, he reminds you that he *made* the mountains.

In everything, the Lord's grace is sufficient (2 Corinthians 12:9). His life is abundant (John 10:10). His love is real and constant (John 3:16). He never condemns (Romans 8:1). He gives rest to the weary (Matthew 11:28-30). He is *for* you (Romans 8:31). Nothing can ever separate you from his love (Romans 8:38-39). He is on your side against the enemy's aggressive tactics (1 John 4:4).

When you are abiding in Jesus, his life flows through you. Jesus, the vine, gives life to the branch (John 15:1). As you abide, Jesus's truth becomes clearer—and you will be set free from the worries that beset you (John 8:31-32).

Slowly, as the fast continues, your anxieties will be uprooted. Faith will replace despair. Belief will push worry aside. Doubt will diminish before God's sovereign presence. In Jesus alone, you will learn to live and move and have your being (Acts 17:28).

You will hear Jesus say to your life's storms, "Peace—be still!" They will obey.

You *know* that God is present with you and cares. You are certain that he will provide for your every need (Philippians 4:19). He promised to do so; he is incapable of lying. So claim your identity in Jesus and him alone, and not in the uncertain whims and fancies of this world.

How Long?

How long should you fast? There is no set limit. It could be that you don't eat for one day. During this 24-hour time period, you seek God with all your heart. Then you break the fast the next morning with *breakfast*—"break the fast." Or you can fast by skipping just one meal. Or perhaps you decide not to eat for several days (you can live for close to 40 days without food, but water is an absolute necessity).

As you fast, God looks at your heart. If you truly desire to address a problem in your life, he wants to help you. If you resist the devil, he will flee (James 4:7). And if you draw near to God, he will draw near to you.

The length of the fast is not important. Your heart's desire to be in God's supernatural presence is what counts. Your zeal to know Jesus better is what matters. Your willingness to submit your will to his, no matter what the cost, is the key.

Start with Food

When you struggle with anxiety, fasting from food may be a good place to start. Be honest with yourself. You often eat, or overeat, because of anxiety. Food medicates the worry for a moment.

But the anxiety returns as your hunger pangs hit. What do you do then? You head back to the refrigerator, only to repeat the deadly cycle. You know you shouldn't eat again. You may even feel a bit guilty. You know the weight gain that you're experiencing is unhealthy. But you can't help yourself—food seems to solve the worry momentarily.

Frankly, that response is a worship of creation and not the Creator. That is what God wants you to address.

Start with a fast from food and seek God during this time. Tell him that you know he is the only answer to your anxieties and woes. Remind yourself that God alone can deliver you from all your worries. Keep in mind that the words "fear not" are spoken many times in God's Word.

Begin with a food fast for 24 hours. Choose a day when you don't have to work; fasting while working is difficult.

During this day, deny yourself food and commit to praying. Let every gurgle of the stomach be a signal to your brain for you to pray. As the day continues, the growls will eventually be replaced with a lightheadedness. Let that be a further signal to pray even harder.

How should you pray? Ask God to identify the source of your anxiety. How and when did you allow this worry into your mind? Determining this will help you avoid such thoughts from entering your mind again.

Once you have figured out the source of your anxiety, bring the matter to God. Lay it before him. You may want to write about it in your prayer journal.

Then cry out to God for his help. Strength. Deliverance. What will happen next is remarkable, even unexplainable. Your lightheadedness will be replaced by a supernatural connection to God. Your spiritual senses will be drawn to your Creator. Prayer will become more intimate and meaningful. Faith will increase. Some have even testified to sensing the spiritual presence of Jesus as never before.

You may even feel and sense God's smile. He loves it when we draw closer to him. As we do, the things of this world grow less important. We become certain that heaven is our home, and that we are citizens of this wonderful place (Philippians 3:20-21).

Your God is a loving Daddy. Your heavenly Daddy not only loves you, he loves to give good gifts to his children (Matthew 7:7-11). And you are one of his kids.

> **When properly used, prayer and fasting are like two fists delivering counterpunches to the evil one's punches of anxiety.**

As you fast and pray, a new strength from heaven will overwhelm you. Anxiety will be overshadowed by Jesus's presence. His light will drive the darkness of doubt away. His glory will replace your gloom. Your anxiety will abate.

You will be set free.

Pray *and* fast. When properly used, these disciplines are like two fists delivering counterpunches to the evil one's punches of anxiety.

For certain problems, both are needed.

If prayer alone doesn't work, try prayer and fasting. Jesus said that in some cases, both are necessary to overcome the enemy's strongholds.

A Personal Illustration

When my son, Michael, was young, he developed a succession of several bad colds accompanied by serious nose infections. First, he would have nasal drip. Then his mucus turned to the dreaded yellow color that alerts parents that something is truly wrong.

My wife, Marilynn, was at a loss for what to do. These symptoms lasted for more than six weeks. She prayed for Michael. Nothing happened. She continued to pray fervently, yet he got worse.

Eventually a couple of open sores developed on Michael's chin, which indicated some kind of systemic infection. She took him to a doctor, who couldn't find anything wrong. He decided to X-ray Michael's sinuses. Nothing showed up.

In desperation, Marilynn then decided to pray and fast. She didn't know what else to do. She was at the end of her rope. She knew that the Bible taught the power of coupling prayer and fasting. She saw that Jesus taught that both spiritual disciplines are needed when facing a seemingly insurmountable problem. It's what Jesus's followers should do when nothing else works.

Michael's ailment had become much worse. And nothing was working.

Fasting was unusual for Marilynn at that time. She hadn't practiced this spiritual discipline much up till this time. But desperate times demanded desperate measures. For Marilynn, fasting was a desperate measure—God's secret weapon.

Marilynn resolved not to eat for 24 hours. Each hunger pain reminded her to pray with faith. To earnestly believe. To pray fervently, asking God to show her what was wrong. To claim God's power and victory over *all* the devil's weaponry. She prayed, "Help, Lord…we've tried everything. You know what is causing these infections. Please show me!"

During the fast, after Michael's naptime, Marilynn permitted him to go outside to play for a while. We were having an unusually warm day in February. Because Michael had been cooped up for days with the infection, she thought a few minutes outside wouldn't hurt him.

Soon, Michael came back into the house, pointing to his nose. Marilynn thought he was asking her to wipe his nose. She had done that many times over the last several weeks, especially as the dripping became worse.

But this time, something caught her eye. When she looked more closely, she had to catch her breath. A partially lodged brass pinback, the kind used to attach insignias to hats and clothes, was sticking out of Michael's left nostril.

Marilynn was shocked to see the pinback. *Where did that come from?*

Marilynn gently removed the badly tarnished piece of metal. She suddenly realized what had been happening during these 40-plus days. The pinback had been lodged in Michael's nostril all this time, causing the infection to grow.

Michael sheepishly admitted to his mom that he had climbed out of his bed one night, climbed up the ladder on his brother's bunk bed, and unfastened a pin on his brother's baseball cap and stuck the back part of it up his nose. No kidding!

Marilynn stood there, half laughing and half rejoicing. She could not believe what she was witnessing. As she paused to understand all that had just happened, an inner voice spoke to her heart. It was as clear as could be. They are words she has never forgotten: "This kind only comes out by prayer and fasting."

When Marilynn took Michael to the doctor, he was astonished. He explained to her that the pinback had not only gone up Michael's nostril and lodged there, but had come very close to entering his upper sinus cavity. That's why they had completely missed seeing it on the X-ray.

The doctor proceeded to explain that a foreign object in that area in Michael's nose was dangerous enough. But because this was a brass object, a "dirty" metal, as he described it, if it had gone into the upper nostril, it would have come dangerously close to the brain. It could have become life-threatening, dripping toxicity into the brain if much more time had passed. The pinback could have posed an immediate danger, possibly leading to death.

The revelation about the pinback happened while Marilynn was praying *and* fasting. To this day, she is uncertain why both added so much fuel to the needed deliverance from this potentially deadly problem. But they did.

And Michael especially is thankful that she listened to God's voice and obeyed what he told her to do.

Fasting can give an extra punch to your prayers of faith. Don't doubt it—try it.

And see for yourself.

Different Kinds of Fasts

Avoiding food isn't the only way to fast. God may ask you to fast from *anything* in creation that you depend on instead of him. That's what idolatry is: loving something in creation more than you do the Creator.

For example, God may call you to fast from watching television. If that has become your escape and what you enjoy most in your day, you may need to deny television for a season and seek God with fervent prayer. During the time that you normally watch television, instead, you take time to pray. In doing this, you are telling God that he is more important to you than television. And your prayers of faith will become increasingly potent.

Or if you drink wine or other alcoholic beverages, perhaps God is calling you to fast from such. Perhaps you are relying too much on drink to help you relax at the end of a day. Or to give you the strength you need to face your problems. When people sip, they often slip.

But instead of turning to strong drink, devote yourself to praying with faith. Say to God, "I'm depending on *you* to address my needs, not alcohol. You are the strength of my life, not drink. I'm certain you will meet my every need."

These days, perhaps the fast most of us need is a break from social media. As already noted, it's one of the major reasons for the increase of anxiety in our culture.

One of the major causes of anxiety among teenagers is their compulsion to read social media posts late into the night. They either set their alarms so they can wake up to check on the latest posts, or they wake up to find out what their friends are saying. As a result, they have difficulty going back to sleep. Sleep disorders and deprivation set in, and they don't do well in school.

Social media is also the cause of much discontentment and envy. We end up comparing ourselves to others. We forget that our friends and acquaintances are likely to post only positive messages about themselves.

We then engage in what my wise dad called "the snare to compare." The only result can be either pride or envy. Either we become prideful because we think we are better off than our social media friends, or we become envious because we think their lives are better than ours.

Pride and envy—both are dangerous. Both can lead to anxiety.

What's the answer? Take time away from social media. Fast from it. For days, or maybe longer. There are some people who make the decision to eliminate all social media from their lives. They often say that they don't miss it at all.

I have a friend who spent hours daily on social media. As he did so, his anxiety problems grew. He became consumed with worry. Eventually he came to realize the connection between his consumption of social media and his negative emotions.

My friend then decided to fast from social media. Not for a day. Or days. Or even weeks. He chose to fast from it for six months. He never turned on Facebook. Twitter. Instagram. Or anything else. Not once.

Plus, my friend decided to use part of his freed-up time to pray. He calculated the hours he spent on social media, and based on that, decided to spend at least an hour a day in prayer.

During this time, he chose to depend on God and not faux friends. He communicated with his heavenly Father instead of people trying to impress one another. He decided to be a follower of Jesus rather than seek followers on social media. He recommitted to finding his identity in what Jesus thinks of him, not other people.

With more hours available to him during his day, my friend also decided to take time to serve others. He volunteered at a local soup kitchen. He started working with homeless men on how to use computers.

Guess what happened? His anxiety began to leave. Peace came into his heart. Life's problems weren't so big anymore. He trusted God to take care of the seeming impossibilities in his life. He found himself by losing himself in something greater than himself—serving others. Life began to have purpose. Everything became more real to him.

Most important of all, his anxiety abated. That's why he began his fast from social media in the first place.

Fasting worked—and it can work for you too.

Final Thoughts

Whatever earthly thing you are dependent upon for meaning, fast from it for a season. Remove it from your life. For a day. A week. A month. Or even longer—maybe forever. Stop your idolatry. Look to your Creator, not creation, for your meaning and purpose.

Pray *and* fast. When done together, the most difficult issues in our lives can be overcome. Jesus said so.

Fasting is taught in the Bible as a needed spiritual discipline. As Christians, we should practice this. Jesus did say *when* you pray, not *if* you pray. And when fasting is combined with prayer, you've got a powerful combination working for you.

But the Bible does warn us that fasting can end up being a mere outward, robotic action. It can become disconnected from a true heart of faith. When you fast in this manner, it's not only perfunctory, but powerless.

That's what the religious leaders did in Jesus's day. No wonder he called them whitewashed tombs. Fasting made them look great on the outside; they were able to impress people with their supposed spirituality. But in their hearts, there was no spiritual fervor.

In Isaiah 58, God's people were forlorn. They weren't experiencing God's power or presence. Their prayers didn't seem to go any higher than the ceiling. They received no answers to their requests.

Confused, they cried out to God. They objected strongly and complained bitterly to him. Yet God still seemed unconcerned. Distant. Silent. On mute. He was not answering their prayers.

The people finally called out to God and pointed to their fasting as proof of their faithfulness. They thought their fasting affirmed how much they loved him. He was therefore obliged to give them whatever they asked for.

In response, God said he was tired of their outward religion, their sabbath observance, and even their fasts. Why? Because they were going through the motions without emotions. Their hearts were far from him.

The Lord gave his people a strong rebuke—one we need to heed as well. Prayer and fasting without a fervent heart leaves you powerless.

But when you put prayer and fasting together with a heart for God, you can watch your problems go away. Together, these two disciplines form a powerful spiritual force against the enemy's fortresses. You must make sure that your prayers and fasting don't become rote words and actions. Meaningless motions.

Otherwise you'll have no power. No authority at all.

Make sure your heart is right before the Lord before you practice any spiritual disciplines—especially when it comes to prayer and fasting. These two disciplines *will* break down strongholds. Deliver from demonic forces. Remove brass pins from children's noses.

And cause anxiety to flee.

But prayer and fasting are not the only counterpunches you can use to defeat anxiety. Jesus has given us some other ways to defeat the enemy.

CHAPTER 6

CAST

When the enemy attacks by trying to place a lie in your mind, pray. Prayer works—it will help you take thoughts captive and usher them out of your mind.

And when you add fasting to your prayers of faith, you will have multiple powerful weapons at your disposal for fighting anxiety. You'll want to use every weapon possible when you fight this foe.

This brings us to the next formidable weapon you have in your arsenal: As you pray and fast, also cast.

What do I mean by *cast*?

Peter is the one who gave us this command: "Cast all your anxiety on him because he cares for you" (1 Peter 5:7 NIV). Peter should know the meaning of *cast*—he experienced the need to practice casting.

Peter had failed Jesus. He had denied his closest friend at a vulnerable moment. Not once, but three times. He then ran away and hid with the other disciples.

Can you imagine what was going on in Peter's mind? Anxiety had bombarded him. He must have imagined himself to be an abject failure. A real loser in life.

Peter's utter failure before Jesus is what makes the words in 1 Peter 5:7 so impressive. They flow from the mind of a man who knew the dangers of carrying around a heavy load of anxiety. He knew the feelings that come from failure—from falling short of his call and purpose.

That's why we should pay special attention to what he taught us.

"Cast all your anxieties on the Lord," Peter wrote. *All* of them. Not one of them should be kept in your palm.

What *Cast* Means

The term *cast* signifies tremendous force. It expresses a desire to relocate something to another place.

In the Bible, *cast* is used to describe the way fishing nets were jettisoned into the sea. These nets were heavy and strong. To throw them into the sea was a forceful act that demanded much exertion. It was not a task for the weak and faint of heart.

Think about a pitcher throwing a fastball with all his strength. Or a quarterback launching a long pass. Or a discus thrower slinging a disc as far as possible. Or someone flinging a knife at an attacking bear, knowing that the force of the throw may determine whether or not he survives.

That's how we are to cast our anxieties on Jesus—with great force! In a specific, determined direction *away* from us. We are to relocate our worries to another place with as much energy as we can possibly exert.

In the Bible, the term *cast* is also used to describe how Jesus rid people's bodies of a demonic presence. He *cast out* demons. This too was a forceful, perhaps even violent, exercise. The demons were relocated to another place far removed from the person.

Think about what this may have looked like. Jesus didn't politely approach the demonic entity and invite it to leave. He didn't approach an exorcism in a casual manner. He didn't coddle the enemy. He didn't try to wheedle or cajole the demonic presence to flee.

Jesus did the exact opposite. He *cast* the demons out! Forcefully. Powerfully. Aggressively. With determination and resolve. He wanted them far removed from the one whom they had possessed, never to return.

There's a day coming when the enemy and all his demonic hordes will be cast into the lake of fire (Revelation 20:10), which God created for them (Matthew 25:41). This will not be a polite invitation, but a furious fling. The devil and his angels will be cast there forever, placed in an eternal quarantine. Never again will they be permitted to ransack God's good created order.

Similarly, we as Christians are called to forcefully cast all our worries upon the Lord. Fling them on him. Anxiety is not be treated kindly or politely. Or coddled or nursed. Or cared for. Or held a conversation with. Anxiety is to be cast away—forever.

Anxiety is an enemy. It can destroy your life. Paralyze you forever. It's like a rabid animal that needs to be killed, not petted.

Anxious thoughts are harmful. They must be forcibly exited from your mind. Jettisoned forever. Given to Jesus. Never to be a part of your life again.

And as you cast your cares on Jesus, you can rest assured that he will take care of them—and you. Why?

Because He Cares for You

Don't miss the second part of 1 Peter 5:7.

You are to aggressively cast all your anxieties on Jesus for one simple reason: *He cares for you.*

Jesus does not want your heart to carry unnecessary burdens. He doesn't want you living on the edge of worry. He aches when you ache. He cries when you cry. He is burdened when you are burdened.

Jesus sees the anxiety that is corroding your heart. He knows it is destroying your faith and intimacy with him. It is not allowing you to be the person he created you to be.

Jesus's heart hurts when you are anxious because he loves you so much. Anxiety was never a part of his original creation. When he created you, he wanted his presence and perfect peace to empower your heart and consume your soul.

Jesus wants you to experience his abundant joy (John 10:10). He came to set you free from worry. It's anathema to him. He doesn't worry about anything. He doesn't want you to do so either. His life in you should calm and conquer life's storms of worry.

Jesus wants his followers to cast *all* their cares on him. He knows anxiety is dangerous; that's why he wants to carry your worries—all of them.

In business jargon, leaders often say, "People don't care what you know until they know that you care." The maxim is true with Jesus as well. Before believing in his promises, you need to know how much he cares for you. When you do, you will excitedly cast all your cares upon him.

What is the starting point for casting your anxieties on Jesus?

The Eternal Father's Love

Your heavenly Father loves you very much! His love is similar to that of a good earthly father but multiplied exponentially thousands of times (see Luke 11:13).

But when it comes to your cares, there is one major difference between the love of the heavenly father and earthly fathers. Consider the following illustration.

Most earthly fathers enjoy playing catch with their kids. It's a way of spending time with them and showing them how much they care. With each toss, fathers express how much they love their kids. After all, kids spell love *t-i-m-e*.

But Jesus does not want to play catch with you and your cares. Once you have cast them to him, he wants to keep them—to hold on to them.

Jesus knows the danger of you carrying your cares. He realizes how much they weigh you down. He understands how deadly they are to your soul. Once you throw them to him, the game of catch between you and him ends. Done. Game over.

Cast your cares on Jesus, then drop your hands. Don't ever desire for them to be tossed back. They are now in Jesus's hands. Walk away.

> **Cast all your cares on Jesus...
> because he cares for you.**

When you cast your worries on Jesus, you have given them to your closest friend in the world. Listen to him as he says, "I've got this. These cares are mine now. Be free from them forever. Let them go. Have faith. Trust me, and go enjoy your life to the full."

Cast all your cares on Jesus…because he cares for you.

How to Cast Your Cares on Jesus

In the pages that follow are several practical exercises you can do to cast your cares on Jesus. As you practice these exercises, you can be absolutely certain that Jesus cares for you—that he wants to help you with everything that takes place in your life.

I have used these exercises repeatedly in my faith walk with great success. Here is the first one:

Practice L-I-P-S

When I start to feel anxious about something and wonder whether Jesus really cares for me, I pray—with faith—the L-I-P-S experience. This exercise helps to remind me of how deeply God loves and cares for me.

First, I imagine myself going to a park bench. Jesus is already there, waiting for me. He has a standing invitation for me to come and talk with him. He loves it when I do that. His heart hurts when I ignore him and try to do life on my own.

I sit down next to him, and he looks at me. I remind myself that he really *desires* this time with me. He wants it more than I do!

Jesus and I start conversing together, talking about all that is happening in my life. This is what prayer is: an honest conversation between me and my close friend and Lord, Jesus.

Jesus gently chides me about some things I need to improve on. He lovingly convicts my heart of areas not yet yielded to him. He reminds me that I can do better. I confess those shortcomings to him. He puts his arm around me with a huge smile. I feel the warmth of his presence and his merciful forgiveness (1 John 1:9).

Jesus then asks me what cares I need to give to him. He invites me to tell him every single one—and give them all to him.

I then imagine myself casting all my cares, worries, and anxieties upon him. Literally and aggressively, placing them in his lap.

Jesus laughs uproariously with delight and asks me, "Why were you carrying all this? Weren't you getting tired of lugging around this mess all the time? What needless burdens for you! I wish you had given these to me earlier. How many difficulties could you have avoided if you had given them to me?"

Jesus is now carrying all my cares.

Next, he leans over to me and places his *l-i-p-s* next to my ear. He says to me:

L—"I *love* you." Jesus reminds me that the proof is the cradle. He tells me that he left the splendor of heaven and entered the squalor of this world so that he could pursue me. Before I ever thought of him, he was thinking of me. He tells me to remember that our relationship is eternal. Then he points to the cross. He asks me to look at the extent to which he went to forgive me, redeem me, guarantee eternity for me. "David, I love you so much. The proof is the cradle and the cross," he whispers into my ear.

I—"I am *in* control." Jesus reminds me that every area of my life is in his hands. He invites me to trust him. He tells me that my burdens are now his. He tells me that he will use all these problems for my good and his glory. He then urges me to have faith. To believe that what he said is true. And to trust that he is in control of everything.

P—"There is a *plan*." Jesus reminds me that it's a good plan, one filled with a future and a hope (Jeremiah 29:11). He tells me that he knew my name long before time began—it is etched on the palms of his hands (Isaiah 49:16). He can't ever forget my name. It's always there before him. He knew the plan that he had for me back when I was in my mother's womb. My life continues to be in his hands; I am not an accident. He has an exciting adventure for me that only I can fulfill.

S—"I *sense* all your worries." Jesus reminds me that he feels what I feel. He knows what I am going through every moment of every day. There is nothing that I am experiencing that he hasn't gone through himself. He will walk with me through all of life's valleys. Even through the valley of the shadow of death he is with me. He guides and protects me and will never leave me. He is empathetic to all my pain and problems. I can trust him.

I literally imagine Jesus saying these things to me. His lips are next to my ear. His words are filled with warmth and affection. I feel his presence and know his love and joy. I sense his sovereignty over every area of my life. He *is* working all things together for my good and his glory (Romans 8:28). I am certain of it.

As I feel Jesus's presence and he speaks to me, my anxieties diminish.

This exercise has been wonderful for me to practice. It has drawn me closer to Jesus more than anything else I've done. As I've shared this exercise with others, many have told me that they have profited from it too.

I hope you find it helpful as well.

Here is another exercise that has helped me overcome worry:

Pray and Walk Away

My wife Marilynn has helped illustrate this truth for me. She suggested that a mailbox is a good way to understand the concept of praying to the Father.

First, you write down your worries in a letter. Start with "Dear Daddy," then write out all your anxieties. Put them in this letter to the Father in heaven. Be specific. Tell the Father all your worries and what they are doing to your heart.

Then jot down the worst-case scenario. What is the worst problem these cares will lead to? Make sure you determine the worst doomsday possibility.

Then end the letter by writing, "In Jesus's name." There is great power in the name of Jesus. It's the name above all names. When you say this, you signal your absolute trust that he—not you—controls you and the universe. Then sign your name. He loves your name; he has known it for a long time.

Next, fold your letter and put it into an envelope. You may want to address it to the Father in heaven.

Finally, take the letter to God's "mailbox," insert it, raise the flag, and walk away. Refuse to return and check to see if the letter has been picked up. You know that if you do, your anxieties will increase. There will be no rest for your soul.

You are assured that the carrier, in his perfect timing, *will* pick it up. It's a certainty. He can be trusted. He said he will come. It's his responsibility to do his job. Allow him to follow through.

The mailbox doesn't have to be a literal mailbox. It may be a drawer. Or a fireplace. You can bury the letter in your backyard. Or put it in a closet. Or a lockbox. Or a dumpster. Or you can shred it into pieces and throw it into the trash can.

It's not important where you discard the letter. Just don't go back to it. Let God answer your needs in his timing, in his way. Choose *not* to let your heart be troubled.

Don't dwell on the dilemma. Or contemplate the chaos. Or ponder the problem. You have given it to the eternal mail carrier, Jesus.

Remember, Jesus promised to rescue you from every evil attack. He will bring you safely into his heavenly kingdom. To him be the glory forever and ever (2 Timothy 4:18)!

So pray with great faith. Then walk away. Fast.

And if you should have to continue battling anxiety for a while? Use it as an opportunity to drive you deeper into Jesus. Learn how to abide in him (John 15:1), how to rest in him and make him your sufficiency—even if he is the only possession you have on earth. Let his grace bring peace to your heart.

If you are waiting on Jesus to come to you, let him show you any bitterness that resides in you. Let him reveal parts of your heart not yet yielded to him. He will. And you will discover that the more you yield to Jesus, the less anxiety will have a grip on your heart.

As you cast your cares on him, you are choosing to walk by faith, not by sight (2 Corinthians 5:7). Once the letter is out of your sight, focus on faith, not anxiety. Don't let your heart be troubled. Instead, enjoy life to the full.

Another Exercise

When you own something and it breaks, you don't take it to a repairman and set up a cot in his office to make sure he does a good job of fixing it.

If the repairman is an expert and knows what he is doing, you hand the broken object to him and leave it in his care. If he comes by your house to pick it up, you allow him to take it away and await his call to let you know it has been fixed.

You can be certain that the repairman will call you when he is finished. It may take some time to figure out what is wrong and to order the new parts. It may even take extra time to ensure the repair won't break again.

Ultimately, you need to trust the competence of the repairman. You have every confidence that he will do the job and do it well. He will then call you when he is done. It's his job to fix the object; it's your job to wait and trust him.

If something in your life is broken, remember who knows how to fix it. The repairman's name is Jesus.

And when you allow him to fix things in his way and time, anxiety will flee.

Pray Three-Word Prayers

Sometimes people tell me, "David, I'm too busy to pray. Life comes at me so fast that I don't have time to write out a letter listing all my anxieties. What can I do?"

I understand the busyness of life. But if prayer is essential to experiencing victory in spiritual warfare (Ephesians 6:18), and it is a potent weapon for defeating the enemy, then how about combining prayer and casting? This is a simple, concise way for busy people to cast all their cares on Jesus.

In fact, I've done that. I've found a way to pray that allows me to quickly cast all my cares on Jesus no matter how busy I am, and it works. Others who have tried this method have experienced success as well.

Here's what you can do: When anxiety attacks your mind, practice three-word prayers.

This is one way to pray without ceasing (1 Thessalonians 5:17). All day or night, no matter what situation you may be in, you can pray powerful, effective three-word prayers. It's as easy as one, two, three.

These three-word prayers enable you to express the desires of your heart in quick time. When the enemy assaults your mind with anxiety, you can respond immediately with three-word prayers that can be lifted up any time of day or night—whether you are waking up in the morning, washing the dishes, cleaning the house, driving to work, meeting in a conference room, or getting ready for bed. These prayers are short, pointed, and potent.

Here is the first three-word prayer:

But God Says

This is a good place to start. Imagine: The enemy attacks your mind with a lie. He tells you that something is impossible—the mountain is too large to overcome, the chasm is too deep and wide to cross, the waters are too choppy to ride on, the journey is too arduous to undertake.

Anxiety starts to creep into your mind and paralyze your soul.

But you know that the problem is not bigger than God. Instead of speaking to God about the size of your mountain, you speak to the mountain about the size of your God. Satan says one thing. *But God says* another.

No matter where you are, you can begin with this three-word prayer: "But God says." Say it repeatedly. Incessantly. Convincingly. If necessary, loudly.

> **Instead of speaking to God about the size of your mountain, speak to the mountain about the size of your God.**

The enemy attacks with a lie. You respond, "But God says."

You can also push back on the enemy's lies with other three-word prayers that express God's truth. Find a promise in God's Word and reduce it to three words. Then cast your cares on Jesus with those three words.

These kinds of prayer are not difficult to do.

Other Three-Word Prayers

Here are some three-word prayers from God's Word that the enemy hates to hear. They cause him to tremble and shrink in silence. They are all based on promises in God's Word. They are easily memorized and can be used like a dagger when the enemy attacks.

But God says…

In your hands.

I trust you.

I surrender all.

You control everything.

You've got this.

God is good.

Jesus loves me.

There's a plan.

There's a purpose.

I am loved.

Death is defeated.

Eternal life secured.

More than conqueror.

People love me.

Life has meaning.

Released to you.

Cast to you.

Carried no more.

Give me rest.

The list could go on and on. Find three words from Scripture that address your anxiety. Then pray them upward to the Lord.

These three-word prayers can be whispered under your breath in a meeting. Or shouted out loud while you are driving. When you utter them, you'll feel the tension in your heart start to diminish. This is a simple exercise, yet so profound and powerful. So focused and specific.

It's a different way to pray and cast all your cares on Jesus. It's easy, yet effective.

Final Thoughts

Find a promise in the Bible. Condense it into three words. Then pray.

Attack worry with these three-word prayers. Cast all your cares forcefully upon Jesus. With all that is within you, throw them to him. Then drop your hands. Refuse to play catch. Don't ever take your anxieties back again.

Remind yourself that Jesus now has your concerns in his care. He will fix them in his timing, in his way. He is the repairman. It's *his* job to run his universe, not yours. You pray and walk away.

When you do so, anxiety retreats. Miracles are birthed. Answers to prayer are hastened. Hope is restored.

And you are set free from anxiety.

Because he cares for you.

CHAPTER 7

CONSIDER CREATION

Anxiety is not solely a twenty-first century problem. It existed in Jesus's day as well. Every person has experienced it since the Fall occurred in Genesis 3.

Why else would Jesus specifically address the problem of anxiety with these words: "I tell you, do not be anxious about your life, what you will eat or what you will drink, nor about your body, what you will put on. Is not life more than food, and the body more than clothing?" (Matthew 6:25)?

People are the same everywhere and that has been true throughout human history. We tend to fix our thoughts on food, drink, fashion, and the future, and we are anxious about what we don't have. We focus on the negative. The glass is usually viewed as being half empty.

Jesus knew how to have victory over anxiety. The battle begins in our minds, in our thought life. That's why he encouraged us to battle anxiety with an active verb: *consider*. This has to do with that which exists and flows in and from the mind. To consider is to pay attention to how we think, to reflect upon an issue, to focus your mind on a specific thought—to contemplate, examine, study, ponder, and mull it over in your mind.

To consider does not refer to a one-time thought. It's a discipline that is ongoing. What are we to consider? What should we focus our minds on?

As Jesus continued his teaching in Matthew 6, he answered those questions.

Considering Creation

Start with Birds and Flowers

Jesus encouraged us to consider the birds of the air. He said, "They neither sow nor reap nor gather into barns, and yet your heavenly Father feeds them. Are you not of more value than they?" (verse 26).

And Jesus didn't stop there. He mentioned the lilies of the field—"how they grow; they neither toil nor spin, yet I tell you, even Solomon in all his glory was not arrayed like one of these" (verses 28-29).

In both instances, Jesus said that to consider is a path to overcoming anxiety. He argued from the lesser to the greater. If birds and flowers are fed, clothed, and cared for, often with greater splendor than humans, *how much more* will the heavenly Father care for the crown of his creation—humans?

That means you and me.

God loves all his creatures. But he especially loves us humans. Why is that?

> **Creation proves God's great love for every part of his creation.**

Only we have the image of God stamped on us. And we alone are of infinite value to the Creator, as evidenced by the fact that God gave his only Son to die for our sins (John 3:16). Only humans have souls and the ability to worship God. Only humans have the good sense to cry out, "To God alone belongs all the glory."

Creation proves God's great love for every part of his creation. He rigorously cares for it. But God especially cares for the pinnacle of his created order—humanity. If he cares for birds and flowers so much, how much more does he care for us? And if he cares for us this deeply and intimately, won't he take care of our every need, including the ones we are anxious about?

Observe Creation and Science

Consider creation—its glory, splendor, majesty, beauty, order, and design. God made everything. And he cares for everything he made. That makes sense. Why would someone create something of enormous value but not take care of it?

Some may ask, "But doesn't science disprove the existence of God?"

Faith and science should never be separated. Even Stephen Hawking, who is often cited as a strong supporter of the atheistic cause, made a surprising statement at the end of his best-selling book, *A Brief History of Time.* In a remarkable passage, Hawking asked, "What is it that breathes fire into the equations and makes a universe for them to describe?"[13]

Later, in an interview, Hawking suggested that the overwhelming impression of the universe is that it has order. He said that the more we discover about the universe, the more we find that it is governed by rational laws.[14]

Consider that rationality, design, and order point to a Designer who authored rational laws—one who created and oversees everything and everyone.

For theistic scientists, science merely discovers how God has chosen to operate his world. God has pulled back the curtain and allowed humans to get a glimpse into how he chose to do things.

Yes, consider creation. It is perfectly ordered for life to exist. Nature is fine-tuned for life to operate as we know it. Where do the laws of physics come from? Why do these laws exist and not others? How can the universe be so perfectly dynamic and structured? The answer: God did it. He ordered everything to be so.

Consider that creation bears the marks of a Designer. Something has to exist originally for existence to make sense. Something can't be created from nothing. There must have been a beginning point, a first cause.

Faith in God does not appear to contradict the world as science knows it. Science has not disproven the existence of God, nor miracles, nor even the resurrection of Jesus. It can't. These matters are outside the realm of scientific methodology and measurements.

More scientists are considering the possibility that behind everything is a God with a rational mind. That makes more sense than the human postulations that there is no God.

As more scientists follow God's compelling evidence, they see the building blocks of the universe. Without the immutable laws that govern nature, science has no footing. Unchanging laws point to an unchanging God. The stability of the laws that repeatedly make life possible on earth point to the reality of a life-giving Creator.

When you consider creation as a means to build your faith, realize it's a perspective that many of the best minds in the universe have adopted as well. Many scientists are theists, and even very committed Christians.

Science and faith aren't anathema. They can be close companions.

Consider All of Creation

Consider the many facets of creation. The variety around us is astounding.

Consider the laws of creation. There are laws that govern time, space, and matter. There are laws relating to gravity, thermodynamics, physics, chemistry, weather patterns, and much more. Where did these laws come from? By random fiat? Or from a rational God? Those are your two choices.

Consider the sun, moon, and stars—how they remain fixed in the universe, operating in orderly precision and with mathematical precision that benefits us. If the earth were any closer or farther away from the sun, we would either burn up or freeze. The sun's proximity to earth is perfect for life to exist. The moon is necessary to control the movement of the waves. The North Star is fixed in its position. It has guided sailors for centuries and continues to do so. Constellations also serve as markers in the sky. The psalmist wrote, "The heavens declare the glory of God" (Psalm 19:1). That's because he considered creation.

I found some of the following information online—information that causes one to pause about God's oversight of his creation.

Consider the timely manner in which bird eggs hatch. The canary hatches in 14 days. The barnyard hen in 21 days. Ducks and geese in 28 days. Mallards in 35 days. The eggs of the parrot and the ostrich hatch in 42 days. Mull over the fact that when a bird lays eggs over a period of several different days, all the eggs will still hatch on the same day—both the earliest-laid egg and the last. Happenstance? Coincidence? Or God's design?

Consider the elephant. The four legs of this mighty creature all bend forward in the same direction, unlike other four-legged animals. This is necessary because he has such a huge body that he wouldn't be able to stand unless his legs were able to bend forward.

Consider the horse and cow. The horse rises from the ground on its two front legs. The cow rises from the ground from its two hind legs. God made both different, probably so we would chuckle a bit at his creativity in creation. But when it comes to differences, God has his reasons—some of which we understand, and some of which we don't. He is so much more knowledgeable and wiser than us!

That is why we can cry out with the psalmist, "Oh LORD, our Lord, how majestic is your name in all the earth!" (Psalm 8:9).

Consider the photosynthesis of the plants and trees, absorbing carbon dioxide, then emitting oxygen. This cycle is repeated throughout the seasons. Nothing interrupts it, providing humans with air that is just right for us to breathe.

Consider that all our needs are supplied here on earth. Our lungs need air, which we have. We need food, which we have. We need water, which we have. We need clothes to wear, and there are ways to make them. We need companionship, and people surround us. For every true need, there is an answer. Coincidence? Or God promising to meet our needs and doing so?

Consider the rain cycle. From evaporation to condensation to precipitation, water falls regularly to the earth. Plants, animals, and humans all need water. God knew this and made sure we would have a constant supply through a miraculous cycle that only he could have invented.

Consider the flowers in all their varieties and colors. All so different, yet all more intricate, beautiful, and breathtaking than any clothes thought up by a human designer.

Linnaeus, the great botanist, once said that if he had a conservatory containing the correct soils, moisture, and temperatures, he could tell when flowers would open or close during the day or night. God ordered flowers to blossom at specified times of his choosing. They respond to his perfect bidding.

Consider the human eye. It is amazingly intricate in its design, but strikingly practical in its ability to allow humans to witness the glory of God in creation.

Consider colors. Think about rainbows. How wonderful that God would allow us to witness them! And then imagine that these gorgeous colors will be even more striking in heaven, where God resides.

Consider music. Four-part harmonies. Big brass sounds and harmonicas. Trumpets and violins. Stringed instruments and woodwinds. Tympanies and acapella solos. Bongos and whistles. Choirs and orchestras. Rock, country, and classical. All came from the incredibly imaginative mind that God has given us, making him the original music artist.

Consider the mountains and valleys. Their height and splendor. Rugged cliffs and chiseled jags. Green trees and forests often covering their landscape like a quilt. Sometimes just dotting it. Sometimes totally bare. Majestic peaks, often covered with snow. And echoes when you are in the right place to call out a word. Or sing a bar of a song.

The psalmist looked at the mountains and asked, "From where does my help come?" The answer was obvious: "My help comes from the LORD, who made heaven and earth" (Psalm 121:1-2). When the psalmist considered the mountains, he knew that the God who was strong enough to make them was strong enough to help him. God's strength would be his strength. The Almighty was nearby to aid him in all his life's problems. Mountains prove that our anxieties are nothing to the God who made the mountains.

Consider the air and breathing. We take both for granted. We breathe about 960 times per hour. Without fail. We need air to live. Do we ever think about this? We should. Air's composition is exactly what we need to breathe and live. Which begs the question: Who made air? Where did it come from? Did it just happen? Or is there a Giver and Sustainer of life who created air for us to be able to breathe and live?

Consider your body. The miles of arteries and bloodstreams running like interstate highways all through it. And consider your nervous system. No matter what part of your body is pricked by a pen, your brain feels it. Millions upon millions of places are known by your brain to exist in your body. Similarly, whenever anyone hurts here on earth, God's eternal brain feels it. It's part of his compassion. He knows and understands when and why you hurt.

Consider your heartbeats. Your digestive system. Eyesight. Hearing. Touch. Sensory systems. Balance. Fingernails. Think about *fingernails*!

Your joints. Sinews. Bones. Movement. Coordination. Balance. Laughter. Empathy. Did all of this just happen from the Big Bang? Or a big Creator?

Consider the love you feel for other people. Toward your mom and dad. Siblings. Friends. Your spouse. The willingness of a spouse to sit by the bedside of a dying or demented life mate for months, even years, until death. (Which is what my dad did for my mom for several years as her health declined from dementia.)

When love is deep and real, you are willing to die for the other person. You would sacrifice your own life for the other to live. Jesus said there is no greater love than someone willing to lay down his or her life for a friend (John 15:13).

Consider love of country. Soldiers are willing to give their lives for others to be free. Where did this kind of love come from? If the survival of the fittest defines how we evolved to be where we are today, how do you explain a love willing to die for someone a person doesn't even know—in a war zone in another part of the world? This love must be rooted in an eternal principle—a willingness to give up your own life so others may live without tyranny and experience freedom. Where did this kind of sacrificial love come from? It's unnatural to a self-protective human.

The answer has to be God.

Now Consider the Creator and You

After talking about the creation in Matthew 6, Jesus then made the leap to the Creator as he addressed the problem of anxiety. Here is his logical conclusion: If God is diligent about taking care of flowers and birds and all the rest of his creation, *how much more* will he care for his own?

Therefore, consider the Creator in relationship to your anxiety.

Consider that God is God and you are not (Genesis 1:1). Most of our problems in life come when we get these two roles confused. Even worse is the fool who says in his heart that there is no God (Psalm 14:1). He arrogantly and foolishly dismisses the obvious.

Consider our rebellion against God. It has caused us to create idols of our own making (see 1 John 5:21)—idols that allow us to pursue our own wants and selfish desires. Our anxieties can originate from our wrongly placed trust in idols. For when difficult times come, they are unable to help. They are useless when it comes to fighting life's problems.

Consider that God is knowable not only in creation but in our conscience—the knowledge of what is right and wrong (Romans 1:18-32). A guilty conscience is real. But it shouldn't cause persistent anxiety. Rather, it should drive us to God, in whom we can find forgiveness and cleansing.

Consider what Jesus has done for you. He left heaven and came to earth to die for your sins. The pathway for a relationship with God through Jesus is now open. We are saved by God's grace and not our own efforts (Ephesians 2:8-9). When we receive Jesus, his presence enters and resides in us. We now know God personally, intimately. As Paul wrote, everything else is garbage compared to knowing Jesus, who first knew us (Philippians 3:8).

Consider Jesus's death and resurrection. Through these actual historical events, we see his love. It is deep, real, and permanent. He never abandons those who seek him (Psalm 9:10).

Consider Jesus's unconditional love. It should consume our attitudes, actions, and affections. It's an eternal love, a precious gift. Nothing can ever separate us from his love (Romans 8:38-39). Absolutely *nothing*! Not even death. We have eternal security because of his love.

As you consider the Creator and his limitless love for you, know that you can trust him with every area of your life—including those you're anxious about.

> ## Your worries are nothing in the sight of the great Creator of the universe.

Consider these great biblical truths: Jesus keeps his promises and cannot lie (Titus 1:2; Hebrews 6:18). You can rest securely in his faithfulness. You are saved from the penalty of sin (2 Corinthians 5:21). You are saved from the power of sin (Romans 6:12-14). There is not one area of your life that Jesus doesn't control and declare as *his*.

Consider this question: How can anxiety reside in someone who knows, trusts, and loves his Creator as revealed in Jesus Christ? Who believes that death is a mere transition into eternal bliss? Who knows this love is the most powerful force in the universe and will never fail (1 Corinthians 13:8)?

These eternal truths should consume and overshadow all feelings of anxiety.

Consider that your worries are nothing in the sight of the great Creator of the universe. They will diminish in view of God's perfect love, wisdom, and power.

Final Thoughts

Are you still feeling anxious? Are you fretting over your life, your future, or the conditions of the world?

If so, make sure you take time to consider creation. If you can, take an entire day to do so. Or even longer. Go for a long walk. Take a trip to the beach. Or the mountains. Or a deep canyon. Gaze at the stars and the moon. Let the sun kiss your skin.

Consider how wondrously God's world operates. How well it fits together, its carefully designed order. And of course its beauty and majesty.

Consider then that the Creator of all creation wants to know *you*. Personally. Intimately. Spend time with you. Oversee your life. Care for you. Love you. Long before you ever thought of him, he was thinking of you!

Consider the cross. The resurrection. The ascension. The second coming. Jesus's rule in heaven. These great doctrines of the Christian faith oversee every part of his created order.

And if you were the only person on this planet, Jesus still would have come, died, been raised, and ascended to heaven to show you his love.

Consider why Jesus came to earth: to die for your sins. To be the Savior of the world. *Your Savior.* To sit at the right hand of the Father, ruling all, including you. Because God is in control and knows the future, nothing catches him by surprise.

Consider this too: If you believe in Jesus, you are seated with him in heaven ruling over all the universe *right now* (Ephesians 2:6). Which means you should also be ruling over your anxiety rather than the other way around. In a sense, you have already conquered your anxiety. Now you need to choose to rule over it.

God is sovereign over all creation and all creatures—including you. He knows what you are experiencing; he feels what you are feeling.

As we learned right from the beginning of this book, Jesus knows that the battle against anxiety begins in your mind. He also made it clear that anxiety demonstrates a lack of trust in God. After explaining the value that lilies and birds have to God, he gently chided the disciples for having "little faith" (Matthew 6:30).

So again, here is Jesus's powerful, poignant question to every one of his followers living on this side of eternity. It is one we all need to *consider*, to think about regularly. Let this question arise every time you have an anxious thought: If God cares for birds and lilies with such endless and perfect love, will he not care much more for you, the crown of his creation?

Answer this question correctly, and your anxiety should fade away.

CHAPTER 8

PONDER THE PREPOSITIONS

Anxiety is an absolutely useless emotion. It erodes your body of health and life. Someone once said that anxiety doesn't address tomorrow's troubles. Rather, it takes away today's peace. Worry is also a relentless foe. It seldom gives up in its attack on your soul.

But you don't have to feel hopeless amid anxiety's assaults. In fact, here is another antidote for dealing with anxiety's arsenic: Ponder the prepositions.

Look at some of the prepositions in the English vocabulary and connect them to God. When you do, you will find a potent faith perspective that forces anxiety to flee. As you believe these prepositions about God, your faith will flourish and worry will wither.

The Prepositions

God Is with *You*

Following Jesus is less about receiving *presents* from him and more about his *presence* with us.

Jesus assured his followers that he will be with us always, even to the end of the age (Matthew 28:20). That means not a day will pass without his personal presence. The writer of Hebrews similarly promised that Jesus would never leave nor forsake his followers (Hebrews 13:5).

God is *with* us. Ponder the preposition *with*. Think about God's abiding presence no matter what you are going through.

As Joshua readied himself to lead the Israelites into the pagan-possessed Promised Land, God told him to take courage and not to be afraid of anything. How could Joshua not be fearful about leading a never-battle-tested group of pilgrims against giants and walled cities?

Here is the reason God told Joshua he didn't have any reason to know fear: "The LORD your God is with you wherever you go" (Joshua 1:9). God promised Joshua his personal presence in every battle, every moment.

God proclaimed this same truth in Isaiah 41:10: "Fear not, for I am *with* you; be not dismayed, for I am your God; I will strengthen you, I will help you, I will uphold you with my righteous right hand" (Isaiah 41:10).

> **God plus you is always a majority in your battles—no matter how large, strong, or many your foes may be.**

Fear or dismay should be anathema to God's people. God is with us, and his right hand upholds us. It also upholds his scepter. And when God raises his strong scepter with his right hand, fear's voice is silenced. God's will *must* be done.

God is with you. And God plus you is always a majority in your battles—no matter how large, strong, or many your foes may be.

Moses doubted his leadership ability. He didn't feel strong enough to lead God's people into the Promised Land. He told God that if he didn't have his presence, he didn't want to even try (Exodus 33:15). God assured Moses of his abiding presence, and Moses proceeded forward.

King David assured us that even though we walk through the valley of the shadow of death, God will be with us (Psalm 23:4). He will protect and comfort us. God's antidote for the fear of death is his promised presence. He will be with us as we face life's last gasp, and then take us home to heaven to be with him forever.

Brother Lawrence, who lived in the seventeenth century, wrote about the importance of God's presence in his book *Practicing the Presence of God.* He believed that God was present with him every second of every day. This knowledge produced great joy in his heart. Whether he was doing the dishes or washing the floor, he was always joyful because he knew that God was with him.

Ponder the preposition *with* in your faith walk. God is *with* you no matter what you are doing or facing. This reality should cause anxiety to flee.

God Is in You

Jesus indwells all his followers. He truly lives *in* the hearts of all those who receive Jesus Christ as their Lord and Savior.

Some theologians call it a union life with Christ. You are in Jesus; he is in you. The closest illustration we have of this on earth is the marriage union, in which the husband and wife become one (Genesis 2:24). It's an inseparable oneness.

Jesus said that he is the vine and we are the branches (John 15:1-5). When we believe in him, our lives become inextricably connected to his— like a vine to a branch. And as the sap from the vine gives life to the branch, so Jesus's life *in* us flows through us and gives us his life.

Jesus's presence is not only with us but pulsates in us. Over time, his life in us conforms us to his image (Romans 8:29). More and more, we think like he thinks and live like he lived. We come to possess the mind of Christ.

Paul wrote, "Do you not know that you are God's temple and that God's Spirit dwells *in* you?" (1 Corinthians 3:16). In another place, he wrote about "Christ *in* you, the hope of glory" (Colossians 1:27). Our bodies are the buildings in which Jesus lives and moves and has his being.

More specifically, union life with Jesus means that wherever he is, we are there too. Ponder that promise.

Where is Jesus right now? He has ascended into heaven and sits at the right hand of the Father, ruling over the entire universe. Therefore, if we are in Jesus, and he is in us at this very moment, doesn't that mean that we are presently ruling and reigning with Jesus over everything in the universe, as stated in Ephesians 2:6?

How, then, could any Christian be anxious about anything? Alongside Jesus, we presently rule over all things. And, by extension, over our anxieties.

Jesus is *in* us. He is our hope of eternal glory. We are *in* him, never forsaken nor forgotten. We rule with him in all his power over every life circumstance *right now*. At this very moment.

Ponder the preposition *in* when it comes to your faith in Jesus.

And watch anxiety flee.

God Goes Before You

Peter's threefold denial of Jesus must have left him decimated. How forlorn and hopeless he must have felt!

But the resurrected Jesus didn't want Peter to live in this defeated state. Consequently, he devised a strategy to restore him. And this plan was rooted in the preposition *before*.

On Easter morning, Mary Magdalene and the other Mary went to Jesus's tomb. There they saw a young man, an angel, sitting outside the empty tomb. He informed the two women that Jesus was not there but had risen from the dead.

The angel then urged the two Marys to go and tell the disciples about Jesus's resurrection. And he gave this specific instruction: "Go, tell his disciples *and Peter* that he is going *before* you to Galilee" (Mark 16:7).

First, notice that the angel singled out Peter to hear this good news. He wanted to make sure that the one who felt the most regret and despair would especially know that Jesus went before him and desired to restore his soul.

Next, note that the angel said Jesus would go *before* all the disciples to Galilee. He wanted to make sure that they all knew, especially Peter, that upon their arrival in Galilee, Jesus would already be there waiting for them.

What an extraordinary faith booster for all of Jesus's disciples! At every point in life, before we take the next step, Jesus is already there waiting for us. No matter where we may go, Jesus has gone before us.

Isaiah communicated this same faith perspective as the Jews returned to the Promised Land after their captivity: "I will go before you and level the exalted places, I will break in pieces the doors of bronze and cut through bars of iron" (Isaiah 45:2). As the people of Israel made their return to the land, God would go *before* them and level the potholes and remove the stumbling rocks in their path.

Jesus said that he would go *before* his disciples into heaven to prepare a place for them (John 14:2). Upon our arrival in heaven, we will find that Jesus has already constructed an eternal dwelling place for us. Death then becomes something to look forward to. Ponder that!

How many of our anxieties would abate, even cease, if we truly believed that Jesus goes *before* us in all our life's circumstances? That he is waiting for us in our next hour? Our tomorrows? Our upcoming weeks? In heaven?

God Is Behind You

Haste makes waste, and hurry increases worry.

That seems to be what Isaiah was trying to teach the Israelites: "You shall not go out in haste, and you shall not go in flight, for the LORD will go *before* you, and the God of Israel will be your rear guard" (Isaiah 52:12).

Wherever you go, Isaiah said, you can go in peace. Why? Because God not only goes *before* you, but *behind* you as well. He is your rear guard.

Why is this important? Several illustrations come to mind.

Football fans know the importance of the offensive guard, who protects the quarterback's blind side. If the quarterback is right-handed, it's the left guard who is extremely essential. And vice versa for a left-handed quarterback. The offensive guard is invaluable and a good one makes a lot of money. He is the quarterback's rear guard.

Military personnel know the importance of a rear guard. In battle, they tell each other, "I've got your back." Soldiers can't see what is *behind* them. Their backsides need eyes.

Read Paul's description of God's full armor for his soldiers (Ephesians 6:10-20). Something important seems missing. There is no armor for the believer's backside. Why is this? It must be because God himself will be *behind* his people as we fight for him. We need his protection there as well, for Satan is like a prowling lion, looking for anyone whom he can destroy (1 Peter 5:8).

My wife Marilynn and I were on a safari in Africa once. Our guide was trying to make sure that we had an opportunity to see a lion. Consequently, he kept looking for a herd of wildebeests.

Our guide knew that every herd of wildebeests has stragglers. They were the weaker animals who meandered behind the others. Lions aren't dumb. They know their best chance for quick and easy food are the wildebeests lagging in the rear—the ones who have no protection from the others in the herd. This leaves their backs unprotected.

If a quarterback, soldier, and wildebeest are vulnerable to weaknesses *behind* them, then we can expect that is true about God's people too.

Ponder the preposition *behind.* God promises to be our rear guard. To cover our blind side, to protect us from what we can't see or know about. He sees and knows. He has our backs!

Jesus's followers should walk with a spiritual swagger. We don't need to worry about our backside because God has it. In every way, every day.

How much would our anxiety decrease if we truly believed that God is *behind* us?

God Is for You

In Romans 8, Paul outlined some profound promises for followers of Jesus. He started by saying there is no condemnation for those *in* Christ Jesus (verse 1). He went on to say that the power that raised Jesus from the dead now lives in us (verse 11). Our present pain can't begin to compare with the glorious future given to us in heaven (verse 18). We know that all things work together for good for those who love God and are called according to his purposes (verse 28). The Holy Spirit in us is working faithfully to conform us to the image of Jesus (verse 29).

Paul then added in verse 31, "What then shall we say to these things?" What things? All the truths that he had outlined earlier in Romans 8. They are realities of the Christian's life. With that in mind, Paul then added, "If God is *for* us, who can be against us?"

What a joyous conclusion in response to all the previous promises! They prove that God is *for* us.

> **When God is *for* you, on your side, you can't lose.**

Our God is *not* against us. He does not want us living in the paralysis of anxiety. He is *for* us. He wants us free from the prison of worry.

King David declared, "The LORD is on my side; I will not fear. What can man do to me? The LORD is on my side as my helper; I shall look in triumph on those who hate me" (Psalm 118:6-7).

God is *for* you. He is on your side. On your team. Helping you. The Hebrew word translated "helper" in Psalm 118:7 is *ezer*. It means "solid rock." Immovable. Strong. David was saying we can look in triumph on those who hate us. That's because God is our *ezer*.

And when God is *for* you, on your side, you can't lose. In the same way that great players always make their teams better, God is on your team, making you better by the day.

And because God is *for* you, you need not be anxious about anything. Ponder that preposition!

God Is Over You

God is watching over us all. He is in heaven and sees everything that happens to us. His eye is on the sparrow and all his other creatures.

In Genesis 28:15, God told Jacob, "I am with you and will watch *over* you wherever you go" (NIV). While in a dream, Jacob saw the angels of God ascending and descending on a ladder. God wanted to make sure that Jacob knew his watchful eye would remain alert wherever Jacob went.

In Zephaniah 3:17, we read this promise made to the Jews while they were still in captivity, before their return to the Promised Land: "The LORD your God is in your midst, a mighty one who will save…he will exult *over* you with loud singing." God told his people he would reign over them with singing!

How can God sing over us when we are in a difficult place? Because he knows that all is in his hands. Everything. Nothing is outside his control. And God is harmonizing the melodies of our lives for our good and his glory.

Can you hear God singing over you right now? Listen carefully. He is. It is a song of joy over his purposes for you being fulfilled. Feel encouraged!

Paul wrote in Ephesians 4:6, "God…is *over* all." "All" means *all*. God is sovereign. He alone is Lord. He rules perfectly. He protects, guides, and directs his people. When we fail and fall, he redirects our paths. We are not invisible to him. God is using all our circumstances for good. In Psalm 121:8 we are told, "The LORD will watch *over* your coming and going both now and forevermore" (NIV).

Ponder the preposition *over.* God is on his throne in heaven. He knows everything that is happening to you right now. He is watching *over* you.

You don't need to be anxious about anything.

God Works Through You

You are the body of Christ in the world. You are his hands, feet, eyes, and ears. Your touch is his touch. Your help is his help. Your life is his life.

And Jesus wants his life to flow *through* you into the world.

In Isaiah 58, we read about how the Israelites became frustrated with God. They were worshipping him and fasting, yet they felt their prayers were not going any higher than the ceiling. They were becoming increasingly anxious and despondent. They cried out to God and asked him what was happening.

God told them that he had become weary of their religious observances—including their fasts. He said that the kind of fast he wanted was for them to share their bread with the hungry. To loosen the bonds of wickedness that held people captive. To take the homeless poor into their houses. To give clothes to the naked. To love their neighbor.

God said that if the Jews would practice being his hands and feet, letting him flow *through* them, "then shall your light break forth like the dawn, and your healing shall spring up speedily; your righteousness shall go *before* you; the glory of the LORD shall be your rear guard" (verse 8).

God then repeated this truth in a different way. He said, "If you pour out yourself to the hungry and satisfy the desire of the afflicted, then shall your light rise in the darkness and your gloom be as the noonday" (verse 10).

Do you see what God is saying? If you give away your life, care for others, and let God's life flow *through* you to others, then your own darkness and gloom will go away like the noonday sun driving away dark clouds.

When you reach out to others amid your own anxiety, perhaps you will find that your own problems aren't so severe. A spiritual endorphin, or a natural antidepressant within you, will be released as you give your life away. That is what Isaiah is suggesting in verse 10.

God said that a cure for anxiety is letting his life flow *through* you to others—especially when you meet the needs of the poor.

Ponder the preposition *through.* Ask yourself how much you are serving others. Then go find yourself by losing yourself in something greater than yourself.

Give your life away to someone in need.

And watch your anxiety melt in the presence of God's grace.

Witnesses Around *You*

Hebrews 12:1 says, "Since we are *surrounded* by so great a cloud of witnesses, let us also lay aside every weight, and sin which clings so closely, and let us run with endurance the race that is set before us."

We as Christians are surrounded by a great cloud of witnesses as we run God's race of faith. And if these witnesses *surround* us, they must also be *around* us.

Where are these witnesses?

They are in the invisible, eternal world that exists alongside this one. A veil separates the two.

Apparently, angels and people in heaven can watch from the eternal world into this temporal one. In fact, the angels—and some individuals—have stepped from that world into this one, as evidenced by the time when Moses and Elijah suddenly appeared to Jesus, James, Peter, and John on the Mount of Transfiguration (Luke 9:28-36). As quickly as they stepped into this world, after a few moments, they returned to the eternal one.

It seems that these witnesses are watching us run the race of faith in this life.

Note a key part of the job description of these witnesses: They are cheering for us as we run toward the finish line. As we become tired or face obstacles and want to give up, they are speaking, exhorting, perhaps even yelling words of encouragement to us. They could be compared to fans urging athletes to victory.

Look again at the transfiguration story. Why did God send Elijah and Moses? Jesus would soon face the horrors of the cross. Peter, James, and John would all face similar trying times in the near future—rejection, persecution, and even martyrdom awaited them.

Did Jesus, Peter, James, and John need heaven's encouragement as they ran the race of faith? Did they need eternity's exhortation to help them remain faithful to the end?

Who else could these eternal witnesses be?

Most definitely they are the faithful saints listed in Hebrews 11. From Abel through the prophets, these people stood fast in their faith and never defected to the enemy. They were heaven's heroes. They persevered to the end, never denying the faith.

Imagine the Hebrews 11 people cheering you onward in your race of faith! They are doing that right now. And alongside them are all the saints who have gone before us into eternity—including our loved ones.

My dad departed this world more than ten years ago. But sometimes I very much feel his presence as if he were right next to me. I have times when I sense him whispering words of encouragement to me—especially when I'm going through difficult trials.

The witnesses could also include God's angels. They exist to care for God's elect (Hebrews 1:14). Might they be among heaven's throngs who are cheering us to the end?

Could these witnesses also include the triune God who made us? Jesus, the second person of the Godhead, prays for us regularly (John 17:20-23). Don't you think that many of his prayers include requests for the Father to give strength so we can keep running and be faithful to the finish line?

In the original Greek text of the New Testament, the Holy Spirit, the third person of the Godhead, is called the *paraklete*. One definition of this term is "the encourager." Might he too be cheering us to the finish line? In Romans 8:26, we read that the Spirit "intercedes for us" when we don't know how to pray.

> **Many are on your side to help you finish the race of faith well.**

Examine your anxiety. Don't underestimate its negative effect on you. Don't minimize its power over you.

Instead, place your anxiety before this cloud of witnesses. Imagine Moses cheering you to have faith. Think about Elijah exhorting your life in Jesus to be successful to the end. Hear Isaiah, Peter, James, and John urging you to believe and not be anxious for anything.

Listen to your departed loved ones as they encourage you to cast off every weight of anxiety so you can run the race of faith more effectively. Imagine Jesus praying for you to overcome the burden of all your anxieties. Hear the whispers of the Holy Spirit calling you to get rid of worry and run strong. And the angels are part of all this as well.

Imagine the wild cheers of the cloud of witnesses. They are all *around* you.

Don't let your heart be troubled. Many are on your side to help you finish the race of faith well.

Final Thoughts

Ponder the prepositions. When you do, worry will flee.

God is *with* you. He is *in* you. He goes *before* you and is *behind* you. God is *for* you. He is *over* you. He wants to work *through* you. And his witnesses are all *around* you.

What reason do we have to be anxious about anything?

CHAPTER 9

REMEMBER

Have you ever pondered God's amazing gift of memory? In our mind, God has given us the ability to remember exact details about the things we experience in our lives.

Not only can we use our memory to recall past events, we can also use our memories to thwart anxiety.

Of course, some of those memories are painful. When they come to mind, our heart winces. Among those memories are failures, broken dreams, rejections, stupid decisions, regrets, betrayals, wrong done to us, and abuse.

But even these past experiences and incidents shouldn't be considered all bad when we remember them. They can serve as reminders of how *not* to do something, or why we should *not* trust someone. Pain can be invaluable when a positive life lesson is learned from it.

Other life memories are positive and pleasant. They serve as encouragements for us to keep moving forward. To believe and have hope. This includes successes, fulfilled dreams, long-term faithful relationships, loving and being loved, places and times spent with close friends, and breathtaking views of God's wonderful creation all around us.

When we reflect on these positive memories, a warm feeling floods our soul. We are awash in joy. We don't want those memories to cease.

As we reflect on positive memories, it's easy to thank God for the gift of memory. We *know* that he is good and his mercies endure forever. We are certain that he is for us and wants our best. We would never want to live even one second without the gift of memory.

Positive memories can encourage our faith like nothing else. Not only do they feel wonderful, but they are like God whispering to our souls, *If I did it once for you, I can do it again.* This infuses us with hope and lets us know we can live expectantly for a new day and a new song. It means we can pray, "I believe that you can do it again, Lord; I really do!"

Remembering God's Miracles

The Parting of the Red Sea

As you read the Old Testament, you may be struck by the numerous references to the parting of the Red Sea. This miracle appears to be one of God's masterpieces.

After God's chosen left Egypt, they were staring at the Red Sea before them. Its powerful waves were crashing on the shore. There was an expansive desert on one side and a large mountain range on the other. From behind, the people noticed clouds of dust rising upward. Angry and vengeful Egyptians were pursuing them. What possibly could be done to save them? They appeared to be trapped, with no way out.

Moses knew the answer. God had told him what to do.

Obediently, Moses raised his staff, stretched out his arm, and exhorted God's people to behold the deliverance of the Lord. The waves began to recede. The sea parted, and two mountainous walls of seawater formed, leaving an open path for the people to take.

The Israelites walked between the two walls and safely passed through the Red Sea on dry ground.

The Red Sea's parting was one miracle. The dry ground was the other one.

But there's more to the story. There was another act to the drama.

The Egyptians attempted to pursue God's people between the walls of water. But after the Israelites had made their way through, the walls of water collapsed on the Egyptians and they were drowned. The Egyptian horses and riders had no chance. They were soundly defeated.

In contrast, God's people were saved. They had been brought out of slavery, and now a new life and calling had begun for them. The parting of the Red Sea stands out as one of the greatest acts of deliverance God performed in the Old Testament.

And God didn't want his chosen to ever forget this mighty miracle.

Repeatedly, the Old Testament writers exhorted their readers to remember this event. David wrote about this miracle (Psalm 136:13), as did Isaiah (Isaiah 51:10).

As did Joshua.

Before entering the Promised Land, Joshua said that it was the news about the parting of the Red Sea that put fear in the hearts of all Israel's enemies (Joshua 2:10). The citizens of Jericho had heard about this miracle, and it created fear in their hearts. It moved the prostitute Rahab to protect the two Israelite spies who had entered the city, and she eventually converted to Judaism.

In the New Testament, Paul wanted his readers to remember the importance of the miracle of the Red Sea. He knew that this recollection of God's power would help encourage Christians in the New Testament era and beyond (1 Corinthians 10:1).

> **Our worries are not beyond the reach of God's mighty hand and outstretched arm.**

All Christians need to remember what happened at the Red Sea. This miracle should be solidly embedded in our memory banks. As we are reminded of what God did for the Israelites, our faith is fueled. God is no respecter of persons. We can rest assured that if he did this for his chosen people, then he can deliver us today as well.

As evidenced at the Red Sea, our worries are not beyond the reach of God's mighty hand and outstretched arm. He loves his children, and he will intervene for them in times of need.

The Resurrection

"Jesus is risen!" This was the battle cry of the church in its earliest years. They knew that if Jesus had been raised from the dead, his claims to deity had to be true. His resurrection proved his lordship over all—especially their fears.

The truth about the resurrection can guide us today as well. Our worries should diminish in the face of Jesus's resurrection. He is risen! He is alive; there is hope!

Conversely, if Jesus's tomb isn't empty, Christians "are of all people most to be pitied" (1 Corinthians 15:19). If Jesus didn't rise from the dead, it's all a horrible hoax. A devious lie. A fabrication that makes us nothing more than a bunch of deluded people.

Without the resurrection, the foundation of the Christian faith crumbles.

But the resurrection *is* true. The numerous eyewitnesses to the risen Jesus didn't make up the narrative. They proclaimed "Jesus is risen" even when they faced torture, persecution, and martyrdom. People aren't willing to suffer and die for what they know is a lie. That's not human nature. We self-protect when facing possible pain and discomfort. The earliest Christians had seen Jesus alive, and that was the pillar that held up everything else in their faith.

Jesus, at the Last Supper, commanded his followers to eat of the bread that represented his body and drink of the wine that represented his blood. By doing this on a regular basis, they would remember him.

Every time we as Christians ingest the elements of the Last Supper, we are to remember that death could not contain Christ—that the grave could not control him. We must also proclaim with other Christians who preceded us, "Jesus is risen!"

As we celebrate communion, we are asked to remember the resurrection. Jesus's tomb is empty. He is not dead. He conquered sin, death, and the devil. Every follower of Jesus must drive this reality deep into his or her memory.

And if the resurrection is true, then nothing is beyond God's miraculous power to remedy. Our problems are petty before the great God of the universe, who can raise his Son from the dead.

Remember the Red Sea. And remember Jesus's resurrection. These testimonies to God's power should dwarf all the worries in our lives.

Remembering Your Miracles

Psalm 103:2 reads, "Bless the LORD, O my soul, and forget not all his benefits." Our faith is nurtured when we remember all that God has done for us—especially in the realm of the miraculous. We should never forget what God does on our behalf.

Most every follower of Jesus with whom I've spoken has a miracle story. There was a time when life was hard and hopeless. They were like the Israelites approaching the Red Sea. Like the disciples right after Jesus's death on the cross. There seemed to be no solution. The possible outcomes all appeared negative. Their foreboding circumstances overshadowed any hope they might have.

But the person refused to give up. He prayed persistently. She believed in a risen Lord. And God broke through the darkness. A miracle happened.

My wife Marilynn and I have such a story. We waited for many years to have a baby, with no results. Doctors gave us little to no hope. Her tubes were irrevocably scarred. The doctors were willing to try doing surgery in an attempt to save one tube and hope beyond hope for a future pregnancy. But they were terribly discouraging.

One night before the surgery, while we were watching a Christian TV show, the host of the show began praying for someone with severe scarring in their abdominal area. A warmth flooded Marilynn's body. She felt like something had deeply touched her—especially where her ovarian tubes were.

She went in for the surgery soon thereafter, both of us expecting at least a four-hour ordeal. After 30 minutes, the surgeon asked to meet with me. A quizzical expression was on his face. Shuffling his feet, swaying from side to side with a degree of discomfort, he said that Marilynn's tubes were "perfect."

There was nothing wrong with Marilynn's tubes! The doctor didn't understand what had happened. This was medically impossible to explain, he said, but it was undeniably true.

The next time Marilynn and I could try, she conceived our daughter, Bethany. Four years later came David. Five years after that came our surprise, Michael.

Astonishingly, three children came from a barren womb. How could this be? We have only one answer: a miracle from God. A parting of the Red Sea for us. New resurrection life was given to us—not once, but three times!

Our God is an awesome God.

And on those days when life seems dark and hopeless and we aren't sure what to do, we look at pictures of our three kids—especially Bethany! We reread old journals in which we wrote about holding them for the first time. We share our memories of those moments with each other. We do whatever is necessary to fan the flames of remembrance. When we do, we are reminded that God is able to do exceedingly and abundantly *beyond* anything that we could ever hope for or imagine (Ephesians 3:20). Nothing, absolutely nothing, is impossible for God (Matthew 19:26).

And Marilynn and I know that if God did a miracle once for us, he can do another one. He is faithful and his love endures forever. Why should we worry about anything?

In this way, memories can make worries flee.

> **The more you remember how God has proven himself faithful, the less power anxiety will have over you.**

What about you? Recall a miracle in your life—a circumstance in which God came through for you. A time when you were in an impossible situation and God showed up. Then place your present worry beside your memory of the miracle. The more you remember how God has proven himself faithful, the less power anxiety will have over you.

And remind yourself: If God came through for you in the past, he can do it again in the future!

Because nothing is impossible for God.

Your Baptism

I'm fortunate to be a part of a church that regularly experiences people coming to faith in Jesus and being baptized. The symbolism inherent in baptism is significant—the new believer goes under the water into a "dark grave" to signify death to self. He then arises from the water to show the new resurrection life he has in Jesus.

Old sins have passed away, forever forgotten in God's sight. A new life has begun. The future is bright and filled with hope. Baptism symbolizes God taking a dead heart and making it alive in Jesus.

When you become a Christian, you are no longer the same person.

After a baptism, I encourage the new believer to always remember this event. He should never forget the symbolism behind this powerful, poignant moment.

Why? Because in those times when life seems dark and hopeless, it helps to remember descending into the water in death to the old life and emerging from the water to new life in Jesus.

Your baptism serves as a reminder that you are a new creation. A child of God. A beloved son or daughter.

God Knows You Personally

The Jews were in exile. Their hearts were filled with gloom. They cried out, "The LORD has forsaken me; my Lord has forgotten me" (Isaiah 49:14). They not only felt that he had forsaken them, but that he had also forgotten their names! In verse 15 we read, "Can a woman forget her nursing child, that she should have no compassion on the son of her womb?"

That's a compelling question. Can a mom ever forget the name of her child? The one whom she nursed at her breast? The one she raised and nurtured for years? That seems implausible. Moms love too much and deeply.

But, sadly, moms can forget the names of their kids. That happened to me, my brother, and my sister.

My mom contracted Alzheimer's disease. For the last years of her life, her three children would enter her room to her vacuous stares. She appeared to be struggling to reach into her memory and recall who we were, but to no avail.

Mom had forgotten our names.

That's why Isaiah said this in the second part of verse 15: "Even these may forget, yet I will not forget you." God acknowledged that moms *can* forget the names of their children. Sadly, dementia can cause this to happen.

But God's memory will never succumb to dementia. He will never forget a name. In fact, in verse 16, he said, "Behold, I have engraved you on the palms of my hands." Think about that. God has your name tattooed on his palms. He looks at your name regularly. When he sees your name, it brings a smile to his eternal visage.

When it comes to our sin, God is an eternal amnesiac. That's wonderful news, isn't it? But he can never become forgetful about knowing us personally and intimately. He won't forget our names—ever! They are engraved on his palms and etched in his heart.

If God knows you personally and will never forget your name, that must mean he knows about all your worries as well. Every single one. When you cast them on the Lord, you can count on him taking care of them. He will carry them because he cares for you.

Never forget that God remembers you and knows all your worries.

Remembering this will help your anxiety to go away.

Final Thoughts

When the enemy attacks you with worry, counterpunch with your memory. Fight back by never forgetting.

Recall God's many miracles in the Bible—especially the parting of the Red Sea and the resurrection.

Recollect the miracles God has done for you. Look at past pictures that remind you of times when God came through for you. Read old journals in which you chronicled God's miracles in your life. Relive with family and friends those moments when a specific problem was overcome by God's power.

Retell these stories to your soul. Out loud, if necessary. Multiple times. Find a friend or family member and relive the memories. Telling the stories makes them become real to you once more.

Remember that God knows you by name and will never forget you. Your name is engraved on his palms and etched in his heart. That's how much he loves you.

Use your memory to combat worry.

It's a potent gift the Father has given you to chase anxiety away.

CHAPTER 10

SING

If you can't control what you think, you'll never control what you feel. And if you can't control what you feel, you won't be able to control what you do.

Anxiety is a feeling rooted in your thought life. What your mind thinks affects your feelings. That is why anxious thoughts will produce anxiety. It's that simple.

Consequently, to change what you feel, you need to change how you think. Romans 12:2 says you are transformed by the renewal of your mind. Conquering worry begins with controlling what you are thinking.

Another weapon you can use to control your thoughts and produce healthy emotions is to sing your thoughts. Fill your mind with positive songs with encouraging words, especially from God's Word, and then sing them. Repeatedly. Make this an ongoing habit.

Music is a universal language. There are not many people who don't enjoy the splendor and majesty of a song well sung and a score well done. Music moves the heart like nothing else.

One secular Motown song from the 1970s suggested that when you feel down and out, you should sing a song, and that will make you well. The next line in the song stated that singing can also make things better.

That logic in that 1970s song is right on. Music can change moods and lift the soul. Secular studies show the power of music to conquer emotional distress and malaise.

For example, music makes jogging and exercise easier, which leads to good weight control and feeling better. In this way, music can make you eat less and improve your memory. It can also help you manage chronic pain. When softly played in the background, music can aid better sleep. It can even improve mental focus and motivation while increasing perseverance when you are doing a task.

According to a recent article, a study says that going to a concert is better for you than doing stretching exercises. Researchers have found that attending a concert and singing songs with others increases feelings of overall wellness, happiness, and self-worth by 21 percent.[15] Imagine that! Twenty minutes of live music and singing with other people can make you feel significantly better and increase wellness. It can improve your emotional health and help you overcome despair. Anyone who has been to a fun, lively concert knows how true this is.

Some experts say that a positive mood change can occur within two weeks when you sing songs daily that have a positive message. Think about it: That's only 14 days to better emotional health—an attainable goal for the most anxious of persons.

A study that appeared in the *World Journal of Psychiatry* found that music therapy is a safe and low-risk approach to reducing depression and anxiety.[16]

Music is also very cost-effective. All you need is your voice and your smartphone loaded with your favorite songs. Add some earplugs and you are ready to sing, dance, and see anxiety greatly reduced.

What Music Does

Music communicates a message that reaches deep into the human heart unlike anything else. It stirs emotions and feelings. Musician Stevie Wonder has said that music is a language we all understand. Author Leo Tolstoy is credited with saying that music is the shorthand of emotion.

Many schoolteachers use gentle, calming music to help young children relax at nap times during the day. Some schoolteachers have played classical music to help calm their students' nerves while they take their tests.

Remember when you first heard that catchy song that sometimes plays on an endless loop in your mind—what is affectionately called an *earworm*? A warmth flushed over your body. You just had to hear the song again. And again. And again. You sang it incessantly throughout your day, and every now and then you sing it again. The earworm easily and quickly returns. You gladly welcome it as the gift that keeps on giving.

Singing stimulates positive thoughts, which in turn produce good feelings that can assist you in overcoming the paralysis caused by anxiety.

Singing Was God's Idea

Music was God's idea. He invented it and gave it to us as a common grace for all.

You might be surprised to know that the Bible has more than 400 references to singing and includes 50 direct commands to sing—not suggestions, but commands. From God's perspective, singing isn't optional. It's an activity *all* God's people should do, both alone and together. Perhaps that is because God knows the many benefits we can enjoy from singing.

"Sing to the LORD a new song; sing to the LORD, all the earth! Sing to the LORD, bless his name; tell of his salvation from day to day" (Psalm 96:1-2). In these two verses alone, we are told three times to sing to the Lord.

Think about all the people in the Bible who used song to express their love to God and overcome obstacles. For example, after the Red Sea had parted and God's people were safely on the other side, Miriam wrote a song about how the Egyptian charioteers had been thrown into the heart of the sea (Exodus 15). Though the ages, different songwriters have taken Miriam's words and arranged them to various tunes. But no matter how her words are sung, they always remind God's people of his victorious power over all his enemies.

King David was a skilled musician. Not only did he play a stringed instrument, he also wrote many of the psalms. Bound together, they became Israel's hymnal. They were intended to be sung more than read. That way, they were more easily memorized. These songs could then be remembered at a moment's notice—whether in corporate or individual worship.

David also loved using different orchestral instruments. Along with the lute and harp, he wanted trumpets, tambourines, pipe instruments, and loud clashing cymbals to accompany the music he wrote (Psalm 150). He wanted everything that had breath to sing and praise the Lord.

David also played his harp to soothe King Saul's ravaged and anxious mind (1 Samuel 16:23). Every time David did this, Saul's temper would abate and calm soon followed. Music helped control Saul's mood swings.

King David also adjured Israel's worshippers to sing to the Lord a new song, one played skillfully (Psalm 33:3). He knew there needed to be a constant flow of new songs that the Israelites could write, sing, and memorize.

When the newly built walls around Jerusalem were finally completed, Nehemiah ordered singers to stand on the walls to celebrate (Nehemiah 12:27). Along with Ezra, Nehemiah made sure that the priests and Levites were in place with the singers so worship could be done right. In fact, more than 200 *singers* were in place so that the people's weekly time of worship included great music. Note that these 200 singers were paid musicians (11:23)—they were hired to sing, sing, and sing some more every week.

Weekly worship for the Jews included lots of music and singing.

On one occasion, when King Jehoshaphat faced a formidable foe, there was little hope he could win. How did he decide to fight the battle? He commanded that his army be led by the singers (2 Chronicles 20:21). Do you know what happened? The enemy fled. The Israelites then collected the multiple spoils left behind.

Could singing praises to God cause feelings of anxiety to similarly slink away in defeat in our lives?

> **Songs of thanksgiving should always be present in your spiritual arsenal.**

When Mary learned she would carry and give birth to the Christ child, she wrote and sang a song called "The Magnificat" (Luke 1:46-55). It was a profound song of faith and praise. I wonder if she also sang this song as she watched her beloved son die on the cross?

Singing songs of praise can help serve as a stress reliever. It's one way to confront worry when your personal peace is threatened. As Scripture says, Christians are to give thanks to God in *all* things (Philippians 4:6). Songs of thanksgiving should always be present in your spiritual arsenal.

Simeon lifted praises to God when he realized who Jesus was. He had waited so long for God's Messiah to come. Finally, he had seen him. In response, he composed a song known as the "Nunc Dimittis," or the Song of Simeon (Luke 2:29-32). The reality of Jesus just had to be sung about! I wonder if Simeon sang this song regularly for the rest of his life? As a reminder of God's goodness to him and all people?

Paul admonished his readers to be filled with the Holy Spirit and to address "one another in psalms and hymns and spiritual songs, singing and making melody to the Lord with your heart" (Ephesians 5:18). Note that the word "your" in this passage is plural. Christians are to sing together. There is something extraordinarily powerful and beneficial about doing this. When we sing corporately, together we replace our anxious thoughts with God's peace.

After observing the birth of the Christ child, the heavenly hosts—a kind of military choir—sang to the shepherds, "Glory to God in the highest, and on earth peace among those with whom he is pleased!" (Luke 2:14). Is there anything more spine-tingling and thrilling than a military choir singing in perfect harmony and in full regalia? Was the eternal heavenly choir's message to the shepherds God's way of suggesting that heavenly music could help bring peace to the anxious souls of his children on earth?

In Acts 16, we read about how Paul and Silas were imprisoned in a dark, dank Roman dungeon in the city of Philippi as they awaited judgment. The chains they wore were firmly attached to a wall. There was no way of escape, and little hope for an immediate release. A skilled jailer was on hand to make sure they didn't escape.

At midnight, what did Paul and Silas start doing? Complain and gripe to God? Become overwhelmed with despair and anxiety? Of course not. They knew that complaining would only exacerbate the problem. It would double the power of the problem: There was the problem itself, *and* the complaining about the problem.

No, Paul and Silas started singing praises to God. In that dirty dungeon, they broke the silence of the night with songs of praise. Together. For at least 20 minutes? Perhaps longer? Maybe in harmony?

Then Paul and Silas's chains broke and fell off. The two men arose and left the cell. As a result of all this, the jailer who oversaw them came to faith in Jesus—he and his entire family. Was his conversion rooted in hearing

Paul and Silas's singing? Did that serve as an important part of his spiritual growth thereafter?

Paul and Silas were freed while they were singing songs of praise. This broke their chains. Is this a picture of what can happen to us as well if we would sing praises amid our dark fears and imprisonment to anxiety? Does it point to the power of singing together? Can singing break the chains of anxiety in our lives and set us free to enjoy life as God desires?

Before his crucifixion and after his last meal, Jesus sang songs of praise with his disciples (Matthew 26:30). Did singing help lift any anxious thoughts before he faced the horrific pain of the cross? Was he giving us an example to follow when we face our own worry-filled moments and trials?

There are 27 different songs sung throughout the book of Revelation. Evidently heaven will be filled with glorious music and singing. There, the music is not needed to soothe the worried heart. Rather, it's for the purpose of praising the One who created all. Why not begin praising God now for who he is, and enjoy the side benefit of seeing your anxiety leave?

God didn't have to create this marvelous gift of singing, but he did. He must love music. Heaven is filled with it, and we will hear it forever. And God must have known that music would help us on this side of eternity as well.

Ponder this: God not only loves music, he invented it. All the chords, harmonies, and different constructions came from *his* musical mind.

Shouldn't we use this gift to defeat all God's foes now—including anxiety?

Fret Flies

My daughter Bethany is an extraordinarily gifted and strong woman. She is the wife of a church planter—perhaps the most difficult task a person can undertake. She's a talented writer and artist. When she speaks and teaches, she does so with authority. She also is presently raising five children, with four under the age of ten. My admiration for her could not be greater.

But there was a time when, as a child, her heart was beset with gnawing anxiety. This was an ongoing concern for Marilynn and me. Bethany was afraid to try anything new. When she felt anxious about something, she would dig in her heels and refuse to budge.

On more than one occasion, I had to force her to do something she didn't want to do—knowing that if her fears conquered her, she would remain a captive to those fears for the rest of her life. These were not pleasant confrontations.

Marilynn and I even came up with a nickname for Bethany's worries: fret flies. Every time a worry arose, we would try to draw Bethany's attention to it so we could confront it. We wanted to help her see the danger of letting these fret flies dominate her life. We hoped that somehow the act of recognizing the problems would help her to overcome them.

But nothing seemed to work. Anxious thoughts dominated her life.

Finally, Marilynn and I had a breakthrough. We discovered what was able to help set her free: singing God's Word. Bethany enjoyed singing, and we would find songs for her that were set to Scripture. We would sing those songs with her throughout the day. Sometimes I would even dance with her, hand in hand, as we sang the song together—sometimes for 15 to 20 minutes at a time.

Does that sound familiar? Singing songs with others for 20 minutes helps to lift anxiety? As we saw earlier, studies have shown that really works. It worked for Bethany.

Marilynn and I also played these songs as Bethany slept at night. She would listen to the words over and over again. Later she told us that listening to the songs throughout the night helped her to memorize them. Then she would sing these songs throughout the day.

Eventually Bethany memorized the words to almost all the songs. They became a part of her vocabulary. She would sing them to us as she danced for us or when I danced with her.

And today, Bethany still sings those songs. They are forever embedded in her memory.

Over time, Bethany's fears diminished. The stronghold was broken. She learned how to conquer her fears. Whenever a fret fly would appear, she would sing it away. Because God's Word was memorized through song and placed firmly in her mind, her faith declarations based on God's Word were readily accessible.

Specifically, here is what would happen: A fret fly would appear and taunt Bethany. She would immediately start to sing God's Word. The fret fly would depart. She would then start laughing, and we would too. The situation was overcome—it was that simple.

The power of song may have been on Paul's mind when he wrote, "Let the word of Christ dwell in you richly, teaching and admonishing one another in all wisdom, singing psalms and hymns and spiritual songs, with thankfulness in your hearts to God" (Colossians 3:16).

Notice the progression in Paul's words about how to use song in your life. The pattern he presented is the same we used for helping Bethany deal with her fret flies:

1. First, Christ's Word needs to dwell deeply and richly in the heart. It needs to be memorized. In this way, your thoughts are filled with God's thoughts.

2. Next, these words teach and admonish you with all wisdom. They are God's truth. They confront and drive away all lies.

3. Then these words are put to music so you can sing them. When you sing God's truths again and again, you memorize them.

4. Finally, singing helps to fill your heart with thanksgiving, which is God's nuclear option for building faith. When you give thanks, you express a trust that God is in control. This, in turn, causes your fears to leave.

When anxiety knocks on the door of your heart, sing a song of praise and thanksgiving from God's Word. Then watch your anxiety leave.

Marilynn and I observed how singing helped Bethany to respond positively to her fret flies. When she learned to sing God's Word, her anxiety lost its grip on her heart. Her worries melted away.

Today, when Marilynn and I go over to Bethany's house to visit, we can't help but smile. Music fills her home. Praise songs to God waft through every room. She teaches her four children songs that are similar to the ones we taught her. They have been memorized by all five of her kids as well. We detect little to no anxiety in their lives.

The grandkids especially love it when Marilynn and I watch them sing the songs and dance to them. We don't mind one bit. First, that's what grandparents do—it's fun for us. Second, their singing builds faith in their hearts (and ours!). And finally, their singing drives away all the fret flies that desire to plunder their souls (and ours!).

That makes perfect sense, doesn't it? Fret flies hate songs of praise that come from God's Word.

This works for kids and adults alike.

Weekly Worship

Let's return to the research we read about at the beginning of this chapter. There is evidence that 20 minutes of singing with other people at a concert can lift anxiety. If this is true with regard to a secular concert, how much more should it be true when God's people gather together for 20 minutes of meaningful, joyous, heartfelt singing?

Churches vary in the amount of singing they do in a given weekly worship service. What would happen if we made a conscious effort to include at least 20 minutes of meaningful, joyful, heartfelt worship in the course of a service? What's important is that the songs be rooted in the truths found in God's Word. Don't succumb to the temptation to worship online, for you will miss the power of praising God with other people. There is great value in being among other worshippers in person. Then the music can be infectious, and you'll find your anxious thoughts being driven away.

Weekly worship should be a priority. Determine to regularly attend a house of the Lord and worship with others. Not merely when you feel like it, but because you know that's what God desires. This habit is one key way you can conquer your anxiety.

As you discover which songs you like most, memorize them and add them to your playlist. Sing them to yourself throughout the week, placing the words deeply in your heart. Once you commit a song to memory, that frees up your mind to focus more on God as you sing. Your song of praise will flow from your heart to the throne of grace without any impediment. God will smile, and you will feel his pleasure in your heart. And your anxiety will leave.

What if you aren't musical and you can't sing? Then make a joyful noise to the Lord (Psalm 98:4). Do your best. Lift your praises to God. You don't have to be good at singing. Just sing!

> **As you get to know other people of faith and sing faith declarations with them, your faith will grow.**

I hope you look forward to worshipping God with others every week. Don't forsake the habit of gathering together with other followers of Jesus (Hebrews 10:25). You will be glad when you fulfill this commitment. Proclaim, as the psalmist did, that it is good to go to the house of the Lord (Psalm 122:1). It's a pleasure to enter his presence and sing songs to him.

Getting together with other believers every week also helps you to overcome isolation and loneliness—both of which are chief causes of anxiety. As you get to know other people of faith and sing faith declarations with them, your faith will grow.

And you will experience God's peace.

Final Thoughts

Music is beneficial to the soul. It stimulates good physical, mental, and spiritual health. And it can soothe the most anxious heart. Many of the people in the Bible used music to express praise to God and conquer giants in their lives.

Singing is thoughts put to music. Sing God's thoughts. Memorize the truths in his Word, and proclaim them through song. As you do so, you'll drive those truths deeply into your heart. Sing them every day, all through your week. And sing them with other worshippers at church.

When the enemy attacks, counterpunch by lifting up songs of praise from God's Word. Doing this has aided countless people through the centuries. It *will* work for you as well. And for your kids. And for all God's people everywhere.

Anxiety need not ransack your heart anymore.

CHAPTER 11

REMEMBER YOUR BODY

After four years of seminary, I was being interviewed by a group of church leaders to confirm my ordination into gospel ministry. I had heard from friends who had already gone through this process that it would be intense and grueling. I prepared myself, to the best of my ability, to answer all the questions that would come my way.

Before the interview started, everyone was gracious and friendly. After prayer, the questions began.

I was quizzed about church history and theology. Pastoral care. About the Bible and the Book of Order. I was queried about my personal spiritual life and disciplines.

I spent a good bit of time talking about my personal prayer life. Prayer had become a very important part of my daily routine. I knew that partaking of Jesus's daily bread through prayer was essential for me to sustain the rigors of ministry.

Toward the end of the interview, I was pleased with how everything had gone. I felt that I was adequately answering every query to my examiners' satisfaction. But I never anticipated what would happen at the end. An older, wise, grizzled veteran of the Christian faith began to speak.

"Mr. Chadwick," he said. Then he paused. "Thank you for your answers. But I have one more question that is very important to me." He paused again. With his reading glasses lodged on the end of his nose, he peered deeply into my eyes and asked, "How would you respond if someone called you a gnostic?"

I knew from my church history classes what Gnosticism was: an early church heresy that suggested Jesus was just a spirit, not human. It was a mystery cult that believed that the physical body was unimportant, even polluted, because of sin. Therefore, the gnostic faith emphasized the spiritual, not the physical.

After listening to me describe the intensity and depth of my prayer life, my interrogator was wondering if I was a gnostic. He wanted to know if I only cared about the spiritual side of life and not the physical.

Politely, I explained my understanding of Gnosticism. Then I assured him, and all the other inquisitors, that I was not a gnostic. I was an orthodox Christian committed to 2,000 years of church history, and I would lead and teach accordingly.

My overseers were satisfied. They approved my ordination.

And here I am, more than 40 years later, having done my best to faithfully serve the church in gospel ministry, still remembering that intense moment. I'm so thankful I knew what Gnosticism was!

Anxiety and Gnosticism

I wonder, though, if many contemporary Christians aren't influenced by Gnosticism when it comes to confronting and defeating anxiety. I wonder if we are so heavenly minded that we are of no earthly good. I wonder if we are so set on spiritual answers that we forget we have a physical body that influences our emotions.

We need to make sure we take good care of the physical body God has given to each of us.

Different Divisions of the Human Personality

The Bible teaches that every human has a body, soul, and spirit (1 Thessalonians 5:23). Each division of the human personality is inextricably connected to the other. What happens in one area affects the other.

For example, our thought life affects our emotions. If we constantly think dark, foreboding, fear-filled thoughts, our emotions will follow with anxiety. That's the way God wired us. Our minds and emotions are connected to each other.

The same is true of the physical body. If we don't pay attention to it, and we deprive it of good health, our emotions can go haywire. The body and the emotions are also inextricably intertwined.

That is why we need to remember to take care of our bodies. We need to do what my wife Marilynn calls "regular temple upkeep."

Your present body is the only one you will have on this side of eternity. Yes, a glorious resurrection body awaits all of us who trust in Jesus. It will be a perfect body without disease, pain, aches, tears, turmoil, or anxiety. This wonderful body will never again face death. Unquestionably, our resurrection body is something to look forward to!

But until that day arrives, we live in the body that God has given us now and we need to take good care of it. How well we do so will affect our emotional health.

Yes, some of us have genetic issues that cause our body not to operate as God designed. Others of us may have sustained injuries that limit the body's usage. Yet we are called to take care of the body we presently have. We need to give our bodies every chance to remain as healthy as possible, even in the midst of any limitations we might have.

The Connection Between Our Health and Anxiety

What's more, there is a connection between taking care of our bodies and knowing freedom from anxiety.

The Example of Elijah

Elijah is considered among the greatest prophets in the Old Testament. God sent him and Moses to visit Jesus, Peter, James, and John on the Mount of Transfiguration (Matthew 17:1-11). What an honor that must have been! Elijah and Moses were chosen and sent by the Father to visit the Son and encourage him as he headed toward the cross.

Elijah was one of only two people in the Bible who never had to face death. Enoch was the first, and Elijah the second. Elijah was taken from earth to heaven in a fiery chariot surrounded by a mighty whirlwind (2 Kings 2:11). God esteemed him so highly that he chose to allow him to bypass life's final enemy, death.

Scripture also presents Elijah as a forerunner of John the Baptist, who in turn became a forerunner of Jesus. To this day, faithful Jews save an empty seat at their Passover table for Elijah. They await the day when he will return to them.

With these facts in mind, it's impossible to overstate Elijah's importance in the biblical narrative.

Yet this mighty man of God experienced severe anxiety and depression. These negative emotions overcame him with such intensity that he wanted to die, to leave this planet immediately. He had lost all hope.

But God restored him. How? Amazingly, by first taking care of his physical body.

A Mighty Battle

At this point in Israel's history, the Jewish people were beset with paganism. Baal worship had overtaken all the people except 7,000 who refused to bend their knee to this god.

The queen of Israel, Jezebel, and her husband, Ahab, led the Baal worship. They wanted all Jewish worship to the one true God to be eradicated. They had already killed many of God's prophets. Elijah, however, had eluded them.

God called Elijah to stand for him and defeat Baal. A confrontation with the prophets of Baal on Mount Carmel ensued. It was a battle of good versus evil. Light versus darkness. The forces of hell against heaven. Two kingdoms in conflict.

Elijah and the prophets of Baal squared off against each other. It was that day's Super Bowl of faith—a confrontation of epic proportions. We read that 450 prophets of Baal amassed together on one side. And the prophet Elijah was all by himself on the other. The odds were not in Elijah's favor. Winning seemed impossible.

But Elijah trusted God, the Creator of heaven and earth. He believed that God was greater and stronger than anything or anyone. He knew that nothing was impossible for God—and that God plus him equaled a majority.

Elijah stood resolutely and courageously against the prophets of Baal—even going so far as to mock them and their gods. He showed no evidence of fear. He walked in the strength of the Lord.

That was why God used Elijah—this prophet possessed a bold,

courageous faith. Nothing scared or intimidated him. He appeared allergic to anxiety.

God went on to win the battle on Mount Carmel through Elijah. He showed himself stronger than all the false gods—performing miracles and showing his mighty power. The 450 prophets of Baal were slaughtered, and a national spiritual revival seemed imminent.

Elijah felt encouraged and emboldened. Hope filled his heart. Confidence invigorated his soul. He raced down the mountain, expecting to hear shouts of gratitude and praise from the people. He was convinced that Israel would finally be ready to overthrow Jezebel and Ahab and restore their commitment to the one true God.

At the bottom of the mountain, what did Elijah encounter?

Greatest Highs Followed by Greatest Lows

Instead of spiritual renewal, Elijah was greeted by Jezebel's ire. The queen had no liking for him. She had just lost all 450 of her prophets of Baal. She wanted Elijah dead. Gone. Eliminated forever.

Jezebel sent a messenger to Elijah, saying, "May the gods do to me and more also, if I do not make your life as the life of one of them by this time tomorrow" (1 Kings 19:2).

A fatwa was placed on Elijah's head—a bounty that asked for his death within 24 hours. How did Elijah respond to this threat? With the same faith he showed on Mount Carmel? With similar courage and conviction? With clenched fists and stern determination, inviting all opponents to come forward and take him on?

No, quite the contrary occurred. Inexplicably, Elijah became afraid. The faith in his heart melted into a mushy fear and anxiety. He ran away in fear. He felt defeated and discouraged. He was hopeless and in despair.

Elijah's experience is often ours as well. Our greatest highs are followed by our greatest lows. Our deepest discouragements often come after astonishing victories.

This happened to Jesus. After his baptism, he heard his Father in heaven affirming his call, and saw the Holy Spirit descend upon him. Immediately afterward, he was driven into the wilderness to be tempted by the devil for 40 days and 40 nights.

After a great victory on Mount Carmel, Elijah ended up running for his life. Stunningly, from his perspective, Jezebel's threat had become greater than God's presence. The Lord never told Elijah to flee. The prophet's sudden departure was not divinely inspired.

Elijah had forgotten his God, and his faith was replaced with fear.

Indeed, Elijah was so fearful that he began running south—very far south, to Beersheba. This was as far south as he could have gone while staying in the Promised Land. He wanted to get as far away from Jezebel as possible—it's about 120 miles from Mount Carmel to Beersheba. Normally it takes a traveler about six days to cover that distance.

Elijah probably ran part of the way, maybe even most of the way. His anxious heart motivated him to run, run, and run some more—as far as he could go.

After a day's journey, Elijah sat down under a broom tree. This kind of tree has many branches, twigs, small leaves, and flowers clustered together. Exhausted, he spoke to God, saying, "Enough." He had reached the end of his emotional health. He couldn't keep going. Discouraged, he asked God to take him home, to remove him from the earth. He wanted to die.

God Heals Elijah's Anxious Heart

What happened next is fascinating. How God chose to heal Elijah's anxious heart is an example for everyone who desires freedom from anxiety.

God wasn't a gnostic when it came to how he healed Elijah. To the contrary, the Almighty showed Elijah, and all of us, the interconnectivity of body, soul, and spirit.

How did God restore Elijah's broken body and soul?

First, God let Elijah sleep. God knows the importance of sleep and its restorative power. He invented it. Sleep was the Almighty's idea. He knows its healing strength.

My son Michael is a competitive swimmer who swims on the professional circuit. He was fortunate to make the US World Championship team on a couple of occasions.

Right before Michael was to leave for one of the World Championship meets, he showed me the instructions that the coaches had sent to him and other swimmers. It was very specific regarding expected behavior and disciplines. Mostly, they wanted good health habits.

One of the clearest instructions was about sleep. The swimmers were told to make sure they got enough sleep—eight hours per night was the recommendation. More, if possible. They were reminded of the rigors of swimming and the need for physical replenishment. Sleep makes the body healthy again.

Athletes need sleep for top performances to happen, and so do we.

Sleep researchers suggest that as you age, more hours of sleep per night are needed. They recommend nine hours. The greater the physical activity and the more the body ages, the more that sleep is needed. It's that simple.

Most of us can remember times when we felt discouraged and a good night's sleep reinvigorated us. We awakened with a sense of renewed hope that we could move forward and overcome the difficulty we faced.

Sleep is a gift from God.

The Example of King David

King David was on a hill watching his son, Absalom, enter Jerusalem and take over his kingship. Betrayal is painful enough. But when it comes from your own son, your own flesh and blood, it's especially sickening and egregious.

How did David respond to this? Psalm 3 tells us that he noticed how many people were on Absalom's side. Many people had risen up against David. Some had even mocked him and said, "There is no help for you from God" (see verse 1).

But David would not listen to the voices of negativity and condemnation. He declared that God was a shield for him. God was his glory and the lifter of his head (verse 3). Somehow, some way, he trusted that God would lift him up and take care of him. He knew that whatever happened to him was totally in God's hands.

Guess what happened next? David laid down and slept (verse 5). He *slept*! And note that when he awakened, he found that the Lord had sustained him. Not only did his faith allow him to sleep, but it appears his sleep energized him. Gave him renewed strength and courage, hope that he could fight another day.

When God wanted to help Elijah overcome his anxiety and depression, the first thing he did was prescribe sleep. Why? Because what happens to our bodies affects our emotions.

Sleep can help us overcome anxiety.

Back to Elijah

After Elijah had slept for a while, an angel awakened him. How long had he slept? I wonder if it might have been for as much as 12 hours—or even more. There have been times in my life when I've been so tired that a 12-hour sleep was necessary. It appears that Elijah was in such a deep, restorative sleep that an angel from heaven had to shake his shoulders to awaken him.

Next, the angel gave Elijah something to eat. He had already prepared a cake baked on hot stones on a fire. Interestingly, the angel had built the cooking fire next to Elijah's head. Perhaps this was so the weary prophet could awaken to a fragrant aroma.

Do you like the smell of bacon crackling on the skillet as you awaken? Or the aroma of freshly brewed coffee? It's easier and more enjoyable to get up to such smells, isn't it? Then there is the pleasant aroma of a bakery early in the morning. It makes you want to buy whatever is causing that smell.

The angel probably knew the smell of freshly baked cake would help Elijah wake up—as well as encourage his soul. This was yet another step toward healing Elijah's anxious heart.

I've always wondered if this cake was the same food angels eat in heaven. Evidently the angel knew how to fix it—perhaps because he had prepared it so many times before. He knew the recipe. Maybe this was similar to the manna God supplied daily for the Israelites on their journey to the Promised Land—a delicious kind of rice cake dripping with honey.

Whatever this cake was, it must have been wonderfully healthy. If it was manna, it surely helped the Israelites remain vigorous during their long journey. If it was what the angels in heaven eat, it must have been perfectly nutritious in every way. We can be sure there is no unhealthy food in heaven!

After the angel awakened Elijah, he fed him good, healthy food. He knew the connection between proper nutrition and healing raw human emotions.

Let's return for a moment to my son Michael's instructions from his swim coaches. The swimmers were also encouraged to make sure they ate healthy food—especially right after they swam. The coaches reminded them that nutritious food restores depleted energy. They wanted the swimmers to be ready for the next swim.

> ## We can't separate the need to eat well from good mental health.

The same is true for all of us. By eating healthy foods, we can stave off depression and anxiety. By properly moderating our food intake, we can build up the energy reserves we need for fighting off depression and anxiety.

We can't separate the need to eat well from good mental health. To do so makes us a gnostic.

Finally, the angel not only gave Elijah the cake to eat, but water to drink. He knew the human body is comprised mostly of water, which evaporates and is eliminated throughout the day. Therefore, the human body needs water—lots of it. Water is also essential for proper blood flow in the body.

Once again to my son Michael: His coaches also recommended that each swimmer drink lots of water. They reminded the athletes that water is needed to replenish the body after a hard workout or competitive swim.

This applies to us as well, even if we are not athletes.

Most health specialists suggest we drink eight glasses of water over the course of a day, using an eight-ounce cup. They say that's one of the best ways to maintain a strong, healthy body and fight potential depression and anxiety.

What happened next with Elijah? He went to sleep again. And the angel of the Lord came to him a second time and awakened him. Then Elijah ate and drank water again.

God still had work for Elijah to do here on earth. God wanted him to select and train Elisha to succeed him. But Elijah couldn't accomplish this next task without a healthy body and soul. That's why the angel made Elijah repeat what he had done. Sleep, eating, and drinking water should be regular, disciplined habits for all of us.

After all this rest and nourishment, Elijah was ready to start again. He "went in the strength of that food forty days and nights to Horeb, the mount of God" (1 Kings 19:8). Mount Horeb is another name for Sinai, which is where God gave the Ten Commandments to Israel. When Elijah arrived, God communicated what he wanted the prophet to do next.

And because Elijah obeyed God, he was once again used mightily by the Lord.

We see no record in Scripture that Elijah ever had another bout with depression or anxiety. Perhaps this experience taught him the importance of sleep, eating, and drinking lots of water. Maybe he started to observe these disciplines with greater care.

We need to follow Elijah's example. He demonstrated how interconnected the body, soul, and spirit are.

The Importance of Exercise

Exercise was probably not a problem for Elijah. He walked from place to place during his ministry days. The same was true for Jesus and his disciples.

Contemporary health experts and cardiologists recommend that we walk a minimum of 10,000 steps each day for maximum health results. Some people use watches or other devices that help count the number of steps they take each day.

The importance of regular exercise as a means to combatting depression and anxiety cannot be overstated. It is one of the most effective ways to improve your mental health. Exercise relieves stress like nothing else. It also improves the memory, strengthens your heart, helps you sleep better, and encourages a positive mental attitude. It can help reduce your waistline, build your physique, and instill within you a sense of well-being.

Regular physical exercise can add years to your life. Plus, it can make your present years more meaningful and enjoyable.

Studies show that exercise can treat mild to moderate depression as effectively as antidepressants. And you don't have to be concerned about the potential negative side effects. Research also shows that continued exercise can prevent you from relapsing into depression.

Additional benefits of exercise are that it promotes neural growth in your brain and helps reduce inflammation throughout your body—one of the major causes of joint pain. It releases endorphins in your brain that make you feel good. It also gives your brain a distraction, taking your mind off the problems causing your anxiety.

Some people like to listen to music while they exercise. That's a positive double blessing for your body. We've already examined the power of music to defeat anxiety. Add it to exercise, and you get another stimulus to thwart anxiety.

Regular exercise helps to relax your muscles—especially those in your face, neck, and shoulders. Harmful headaches often abate. Simple moments of rest and relaxation are increased. Sleep is improved. And the immune system grows stronger.

If you are not presently exercising, start off with a few minutes a day. If possible, schedule your exercise at a time during the day when you feel most energized. Either walk or jog. Do low-impact exercises. Take a class with people who are like you. That way, you won't feel intimidated about starting to exercise.

Increase your exercise regimen as you feel more energized. If you need to stop for five or ten minutes, do so. That's fine. The key is to keep trying. The more you exercise, the more you will want to do so. Just keep at it.

Maybe you like dancing. Or you can jog around the track during your kids' soccer practices. You could ride a bike. Or work in your garden. Just get active. Move the body God has given you. Again, it's the only one you'll have on this side of eternity.

Reward yourself when you succeed. Take an extended hot shower or bath. Or watch your favorite television show or movie.

The goal to work toward is around 30 minutes per day for five days a week. Studies show that when you exercise this much, you can experience a significant reduction in anxiety and depression.

Once you start, don't give up. Don't be a gnostic. Realize that your body and emotions are connected. When you care for one, you are caring for the other.

Final Thoughts

No thoughtful Christian ever wants to be accused of being a gnostic theologically. It's heresy. A faithful follower of Jesus can't view life that way.

Nor should we be a gnostic in how we live our lives and combat anxiety. We need to remember that our bodies are fearfully and wonderfully made (Psalm 139:14).

> **God needs people with healthy minds, bodies, and emotions to accomplish his purposes.**

Anxiety grows if we don't realize that we are body, soul, and spirit. All are interlocked together. If we fail to understand the interconnectivity of our bodies, then our negative emotions will rule the day.

Remember that there are practical things you can do daily with your body to help you defeat negative emotions like depression and anxiety: You must learn to sleep enough hours, eat well, and drink lots of water. You must also exercise.

Be sure to practice these disciplines regularly. God needs people with healthy minds, bodies, and emotions to accomplish his purposes. If we're not healthy, we could end up being paralyzed by anxiety and depression.

Elijah discovered this to be true.

We need to as well.

CHAPTER 12

DEVELOP AN ETERNAL PERSPECTIVE

How much would our anxiety diminish if we developed an eternal perspective on everything that happens to us—if we looked at our problems from God's point of view?

"If then you have been raised with Christ, seek the things that are above, where Christ is, seated at the right hand of God" (Colossians 3:1). Jesus's followers have died with him *and* been raised with him. This is a mind-boggling reality when contemplated and rightly understood.

This reality is what Paul exhorted Christians to *seek*. We are to pursue the things that are above, where Jesus is seated.

Jesus has all power and authority over everything in the world. All belongs to him and exists for him. He is seated at the right hand of God, in a position of absolute control. In this position, he not only rules the world, but regularly makes intercession for his followers (Romans 8:34).

Right now, if you are a follower of Jesus, know that he is praying for you. Picture him on his knees, making your requests known to the Father.

In addition, the Bible says that Christians are seated next to Jesus in heaven, right beside his throne, ruling with him (Ephesians 2:6). What an amazing truth! Believers in Jesus reign *right now*, with him, over everything that is happening in this world.

Jesus's followers are to seek a deeper knowledge of Jesus himself. We are called to fully understand what it means to live unabashedly with and for him. We need to seek first his kingdom and live a life that glorifies his name.

After declaring who Jesus is and our position with him, Paul then exhorted all believers to think in accordance with who we are, to view life from God's eternal perspective: "Set your minds on things that are above, not on things that are on earth" (Colossians 3:2).

Set your minds on things that are above. It's an imperative, not a suggestion.

Paul wrote these poignant words as a reminder for all Christians to control their thought life. To think as God wants us to think. To look at life from his point of view.

We become confused when we look at life from this earth's point of view. Our problems become blurry. Out of focus. Out of control. Hate seems to win. Evil defeats good. Division conquers unity.

Consequently, unbelief heightens…and anxiety rages within.

But when we who are followers of Jesus look at life from heaven's point of view, we possess a powerful antidote to anxiety. Inner peace is the result—a supernatural peace that surpasses all understanding. It's a peace that flows from heaven's throne to our hearts.

> **An eternal perspective means that we believe God is in control of everything— and we let that truth permeate our thoughts and actions.**

Go Higher

Paul exhorted his readers to go higher in their faith, to go to Jesus's throne. Look at your problems the way he views them—from above. He is over them. They pose no problem for him. They are under his feet, and he crushes them all.

An eternal perspective means that we believe God is in control of everything—and we let that truth permeate our thoughts and actions. He oversees all. He is sovereign over history. He manages everything in our lives as well, both the good and the bad. Nothing is outside his jurisdiction.

Christians are not citizens of this earth, but of heaven (Philippians 3:20). There is only one kingdom we belong to, and that kingdom belongs to Jesus. He is the King of his kingdom, and we are his loyal citizens. He rules his kingdom, and that's the foundation of our faith and trust.

If we know that our sovereign Lord cares for us, why be afraid? Why worry about anything? That's what it means to have an eternal perspective.

The Bible tells us that Jesus is working all things together for our good and his glory (Romans 8:28). All things, both great and small, are under his purview. He is even able to use evil for good (Genesis 50:20). That's the reason we can give thanks in *all* things, even bad things (1 Thessalonians 5:18).

Every single second of our lives was mapped out by God before the world was created. He even knew us by name before the world was formed. Jesus is not surprised by anything but is ahead of everything. No matter what happens to us, he is already there waiting for us. In his lovingkindness, he meets us at every point of need.

We are to possess a childlike faith that trusts God at all times. He is a loving daddy, intimate and concerned about every area of our lives. We trust that when we hold up our arms, he will lift us up, hold, and care for us. He hears our every request as a loving father listens to the requests of his children. He knows our weaknesses and encourages our strengths.

Jesus wants us to come to him when we are heavy of heart. He wants to carry our burdens and lift us up. When we turn our concerns over to him, our burdens become lighter because he is carrying them.

Jesus will never let us go. He dabs every tear. He cries with us. He knows everything we are going through. He was fully human and tempted as we are. Through every trial, he always chose to obey the Father's will—which is what he desires us to do as well. Living out this kind of obedience will bring us great joy.

Jesus truly cares for us—he really does. The cross and resurrection prove it. His love for us will never end. He also has a plan for us. It's a good plan, one filled with a future and a hope. He hates how sin has ransacked his once-perfect created order and how much it has hurt us. He doesn't want us to live as slaves to sin. He came to earth to set us free from the ravages of sin so that we could experience lives of abundant joy, not despair and anxiety.

Jesus despises death. That's the ultimate reason he came to earth: to assure us that death is not the final word. Jesus *is* the resurrection and the life. If we believe in him and place our faith in him, we have the gift of eternal life and will never die. For those of us who are believers, death has lost its sting. It has no power over us. The fear of death has lost its grip on our souls.

When you die, so what? You immediately go to be with Jesus. Death is the gateway to life. Because of Jesus, the worst thing that could ever happen to you has become the best thing that could ever happen to you.

Our resurrection hope changes everything about the way we live. It gives us an eternal perspective. We no longer need to be anxious about the days of our lives because we know that all days are overseen by the Ancient of Days. He created the days, weeks, months, and years. "In the beginning, God created the heavens and the earth" is a truth embedded in our minds (Genesis 1:1).

It's God's world. He made it. He controls it. He has given us the privilege of living in it. For these reasons, all praise and glory belong to him alone.

God made us and controls us as well. If even one atom in our lives is outside his sovereign control, then everything is outside his sovereign control. But that's not the case. We can rest in him. He is God, and we are not.

We are called to fix our minds on things above, to develop an eternal perspective. When we believe that God controls everything, including our lives, we start looking at everything from his viewpoint. From a heavenly perspective. Through *his* lenses alone.

A Historical Example

God told the Israelites that if they obeyed his law, they would know great blessings. They would live in the Promised Land forever. To the contrary, if they disobeyed him, they would be taken into captivity by a foreign power. God's judgment would come upon them (Deuteronomy 30:15-18).

For centuries, the Israelites refused to obey God. His patience finally ran out. Their persistent disobedience brought pagan Babylon and God's judgment upon them. First the northern kingdom was conquered by Assyria. Then the southern kingdom was taken into captivity by Babylon—as God said would happen—for 70 years.

Nebuchadnezzar was king when Babylon conquered Israel's southern kingdom. He was wicked beyond words. He ruled with an iron fist and despotic nature. His reign was marked by cruelty and intimidation. He was known to lead captives from their homeland with fishhooks in their mouths, symbolizing their status as slaves. He cut people in two if they displeased him in any way. This punishment served as a dire warning to all not to cross him, or theirs would be a similar fate.

Nebuchadnezzar was not a good person.

Yet astonishingly, the Bible calls Nebuchadnezzar God's "servant" (Jeremiah 43:10). This evil, cruel, wicked, godless king was called a servant of God himself. How can this be?

It's simple: God sovereignly chose to use Nebuchadnezzar as his instrument of judgment against his people. Could God have chosen another person? Of course. God can do anything he wants. But he chose Nebuchadnezzar to bring divine judgment upon his children. That's his right as King of the universe.

God was using this wicked king for his ultimate purposes. He controls all rulers (Daniel 2:21-22). He lifts up and abases whomever he chooses to. His overarching providence controls all.

History is God's story. He began it, and he will end it. He is the Alpha and the Omega. Not one thing is outside his understanding and oversight.

God is in control of our story as well. In fact, our story is within *his* story. He knows. He cares. When we don't understand what is happening to us, it's because we don't possess his heavenly perspective. We aren't high enough.

But should we dare to elevate our vision and look down at our lives from an eternal vantage point, from God's throne of grace, our problems will shrink. Faith will grow. Trust will increase.

And anxiety will shrivel.

A Personal Example

I had just finished playing my third year in the European professional basketball league. I loved playing this game. It had been my life's passion since I was a kid. Having reached a relatively high level of success, I enjoyed being able to play for as long as possible. My body was still healthy. So, I signed a contract to play for a fourth year.

Upon arriving home for the summer, I decided to work at the University of North Carolina basketball camp. While there, I experienced a growing sense that I needed to start thinking about something other than basketball. I knew that I couldn't play forever. But, strangely, the feeling of urgency about thinking ahead intensified even though I'd signed to play another season.

Then the telegram came. It was from my team in Europe. They had decided to void my contract and sign a different player. I knew who they were going to sign in my place. I had played against him. He was truly good—a terrific player. If I had been in their shoes, I'd have voided my contract and signed him as well!

Yes, I was disappointed. My days of playing competitive basketball at a high level had abruptly come to an end. Poof! Gone in a moment.

After a few hours, reality finally hit me. What do I do now? What career path do I pursue? I had started wondering if I needed to think about the future, and now, the future was staring me in the face.

I sought counsel from my college basketball coach, Dean Smith. I asked him if he knew of anything I could possibly do. Empathetically, he said no. He then encouraged me to call John Lotz, who was the assistant coach at North Carolina when I played and was now the head coach at the University of Florida. Because I had played high school ball in Orlando, Florida, Coach Smith wondered if John might have something for me.

After the basketball camp finished, I went home to Orlando. Upon arrival, I immediately picked up the phone and called John. I told him about what had happened and asked him if he could help me in any way.

John said that regrettably, he wasn't able to help. He had already promised his graduate assistantship to another person, a position that would have been perfect for me. He told me that if the situation changed, he would give me a call. I thanked him, and we hung up.

My anxiety grew. I didn't know what to do. I experienced a sleepless night, tossing and turning, trying to figure out my next steps. Worry became a close friend. Mom and Dad tried to counsel me, but there was little help they could give me. I was on my own.

The next day, the phone rang. It was John Lotz. With some excitement in his voice, he told me that the person who was going to serve in the graduate assistantship had just walked into his office and told him that he wanted to pursue a different career path. The position was mine if I wanted it.

I grabbed the opportunity. An answer of *yes* excitedly flowed from my lips!

I asked John when he needed to meet personally with me. He said immediately. I didn't hesitate. I jumped into my car and drove to Gainesville, Florida.

I met with John. He told me that he was excited I could join his staff, but there was a problem. It was already July, and to be a graduate assistant, I needed to be in graduate school. He asked me what course of study I wanted to pursue. Most of the schools had already accepted their quota.

I hadn't given this one iota of thought. I had been a broadcasting major in my undergraduate studies. I loved speaking and felt comfortable doing so. But long ago, I had decided I didn't want to pursue that as a life profession.

I thought for a few moments. I knew that I enjoyed helping people. Friends frequently came to me for help and insights into their problems. Almost without thinking, I blurted out, "Well, John, maybe I should pursue a graduate degree in counseling."

John paused for a moment. Then a huge grin crossed his face. "Well," he said, "that's very interesting. The head of the graduate counseling program is also the head of the Gainesville Tip-Off Club...and one of my closest friends. Let me give him a call right now."

The chairman of the program came over to John's office. He informed me that for every 100 applications they received, they accepted only one applicant. That felt ominous. He paused. There was an awkward silence. Anxiety arose in my heart.

After all, it was already July. That meant I was applying very late. *This isn't going to work,* I thought to myself. *What will I do now?*

The chairman glanced at me, then at John, and said, "Let me see what I can do." He instructed me to get my transcript from UNC and letters of recommendation to him as soon as possible. I did. He was able to get me admitted. I began classes in late August. There was a whirlwind of activity as my application made its way through the approval process, but I was admitted to the program.

Looking back, I can see how God's hand guided me through that time. He knew I needed to be in Gainesville. He oversaw John and the graduate counseling chair being good friends. He had all the details in his hands.

After two years, I earned my graduate degree in counseling from the University of Florida. I learned how to listen to and care for people, including those who were going through deep crises.

There's more: During my last month of study, God went into action again. He began to write the next chapter in my life. Dramatically, he called me into ministry. With tear-filled eyes, I surrendered everything to God's will. This had been the Father's will for me before the world was ever created.

That was a transition I'll never forget. And I could see God's plan for me continuing to unfold.

I entered seminary with an undergraduate degree in communications and a graduate degree in counseling. What are the two most important skills a pastor needs to have a successful ministry? To be able to talk and to listen. I had both as a part of my education before seminary.

God went before me. He guided my every step. He had been preparing me for this stage of my life. He had for me a glorious future filled with hope. All of this was based on a plan he had authored before the world was created.

If I had developed that kind of eternal perspective earlier in my life, how much anxiety could I have avoided?

Also, if I hadn't spent those two years in Gainesville, I would have not been in seminary at the right time to meet my wife on a blind date at the end of my first year. Out of nowhere, we met. Our coming together was an amazing, sanctified, serendipitous event led by God's grace.

And now, more than 40 years later, I look at our three kids and when they were born. And I look at our grandkids and when they were born. And I think of the future generations that will enter this world because of the love and commitment Marilynn and I have for one another and Jesus.

All these amazing, wonderful people would never have entered this world if that European basketball team had not chosen to void my contract and sign another player. If I had returned and played a fourth season.

At the time it happened, being let go by the team seemed awful. It created great anxiety. But from God's perspective, being released was the best thing that ever could have happened to me. He knew what he was doing. My story was within God's story.

History is *his* story.

Think on the things that are above. Develop an eternal perspective on your life. There's a big plan unfolding. God has everything covered. He knows what he is doing. It's *his* plan.

Surrender. Trust him. Believe that he is controlling your life.

When you do, your anxiety will go away.

While You Wait

Waiting can be excruciating and agonizing—especially when we don't know what the outcome will be. While we wait, we hope for the best thing that could happen and worry about the worst.

Waiting can be like walking into a dark room. You walk very slowly, feeling your way along to the next step, hoping you won't stub your toe or fall. In the meantime, we ask God, "How long, O Lord? Will you forget me forever? How long will you hide your face from me? How long must I take counsel in my soul and have sorrow in my heart all the day?" (Psalm 13:1-2).

We love it when God immediately says *yes* to a prayer request. We aren't quite as excited when the answer is *wait.*

Anxiety tends to exacerbate when we have to wait on the Lord. There is a desire that's on our heart. We sense that God has promised something to us. We make our requests known to him. We hope for an affirmative answer. We pray fervently, as the Bible commands.

Sometimes we even try to help God fulfill the plan in our own strength without consulting with him. Like Abraham did when he took Hagar as a second wife and conceived Ishmael, thus setting up many centuries of future problems.

When weeks, months, and years go by without a response from God, we wonder, *Has God forgotten about me? Does he not care?*

Some of God's greatest saints have been forced to wait a long time for an answer. Abraham had to wait 25 years for the promised child, Isaac. Joseph had to wait 22 years before his vision from God was fulfilled. Moses was in the wilderness for 40 years before God's call came to him. David waited many years before he became king. Even Jesus had to wait until he was 30 years old before he began his earthly ministry.

Though waiting is hard, it serves as a faith builder. Waiting has a way of revealing the latent idols in our lives. It exposes the things of this world that have taken priority over God.

An idol is simply anything other than God that we seek in an attempt to find joy, peace, meaning, and purpose. Idols are where we invest our time, talents, and resources. They motivate our choices. Because our minds are focused on them, they influence our moods and emotions.

And they cause anxiety. Worry is often the result of a mind fixed on an idol.

When a Wall Street executive jumps to his death because of a market crash, it means he died because of an idol. He or she didn't believe that God could pick up the pieces and help restore his or her life.

When a father watches his son fail in a sport and he becomes anxious and depressed, he has made his son's success an idol. It could be that he is living through his son to accomplish what he never did. Nevertheless, it's an idol.

When a single person puts his or her hopes into finding the right marriage partner but that person never materializes and anxiety grows, then that hoped-for person has become an idol. No person (creation) can ever meet the deepest longings of our heart. Only the Creator can.

> **Ultimately, faith in God is not in what he will do for us, but in himself alone.**

We were all created to worship. God has placed eternity in our hearts (Ecclesiastes 3:11). The question is, What will we worship? Worshipping creation only makes our anxiety increase. By contrast, worshipping God gives us peace.

Most of us will never fall prey to rampant disobedience. Rather, we are more prone to give in to the subtle and deceptive nature of idols. They can be good desires that end up taking too much priority in our lives.

That's why putting an idol to death is necessary for defeating anxiety. Another word for this is *mortification*—that is, putting an idol on the altar and killing it so it no longer has hold over us. In doing this, we give up our right to do whatever we want and trust God to do what he wants—in his way and his time.

Ultimately, faith in God is not in what he will do for us, but in himself alone. Faith doesn't hold on to a particular outcome or desire, but to God himself.

Waiting on the Lord, then, becomes a powerful way to defeat anxiety. It forces us to cling to him alone. Each day allows us to make a fresh faith confession of unabashed trust in God—a new proclamation of total surrender to him.

Final Thoughts

Perhaps one of the reasons God is forcing you to wait is to forge an even deeper faith in you. To teach you how to hear his voice better. To deepen your commitment to him. To prepare you for the ministry call he has on your life—much like he did to me.

God wants to conform you to Jesus's image (Romans 8:29). That's the reason he created you, and his goal for your life. This transformation happens from the inside out. Once Jesus invades your heart, you start to live as he did. You become his ambassador wherever you go. You are his hands, feet, and mouth to those around you.

Waiting has a way of diminishing the lusts of the flesh and wrong desires of the heart. God is much more concerned with who you are and who you will become than what you possess. He doesn't care about what you own, but who owns you.

God knows what you need. He alone sees all of history—from the beginning to the end. He alone knows the future. He holds it in his hands. He has an eternal perspective, and we don't. That's why it's vital for you to set your mind on things above—on him who sits on the throne of heaven. Who knows all and is all.

Leave the temporal and pursue the eternal.

Repent of your desire to control your life. Relinquish that completely to God. Pry your puny fingers loose from any and all earthly desires. Go into a faith freefall, knowing you are falling into the hands of the one who loves and created you. Who died to give you the gift of eternal life, a gift received solely by his grace, mercy, and kindness.

Trust the Lord today. Make him the master passion of your life. He knows all. He controls all. Let him control you. He wants to be your all in all. Your sufficiency. Your reason for living. He desires to hear you whisper to him that he is enough. That nothing in this world can ever bring you lasting satisfaction except him.

Set your mind on things above. Develop an eternal perspective.

And watch anxiety flee.

CHAPTER 13

GET GOOD TEAMMATES

t's not good for people to be alone. God said so (Genesis 2:18). We were
created to exist with one another in community.

Aloneness is a major cause of anxiety. Through social media, people
hide behind a screen from human engagement. Face-to-face, eye-to-eye,
and touch-to-touch encounters happen less frequently. The less true interaction we have, the more anxiety will increase.

That's why we must have good teammates to walk with us in life. We
need people who will come alongside us to build our faith and give us
words of encouragement—especially when we don't think we can take
another step. We need friends who will fill our minds with hopeful messages when worries come our way.

My college basketball coach said, "If you want to play an individual
sport, play tennis. Basketball is a team sport. You can't succeed unless you
play together. You need one another to win."

We need one another to win in life as well.

There is no *I* in T-E-A-M. Each player on a team must do his part for
the team to win. Whether it's a superstar or seldom-used reserve, each
player is required to do what he does best for the entire team to succeed.

> **Positive words can ignite faith and give
> you the confidence to defeat giants.**

We need good teammates to walk alongside us and speak words of life
that help ward off anxiety. Life and death begin with the tongue (Proverbs

18:21). Negative words can sear your soul for a lifetime. Positive words can ignite faith and give you the confidence to defeat giants.

When you are walking along a dark path and you're not sure of your next step, you want to have someone next to you pointing out potential hazards. When a friend watches out for you, life is easier.

The book of Proverbs is filled with different admonishments about the importance of positive friendships:

Proverbs 13:20: "Whoever walks with the wise becomes wise, but the companion of fools will suffer harm."

Proverbs 18:24: "A man of many companions may come to ruin, but there is a friend who sticks closer than a brother."

Proverbs 19:20: "Listen to advice and accept instruction, that you may gain wisdom in the future."

Who is speaking words of faith into your life? Do you have teammates who encourage you? Or are your friends forever tearing you down and causing more worry in your mind?

Hungry lions look for the weakest and most isolated animal in a herd to attack and devour—as does the evil one when it comes to people (1 Peter 5:8). Have you isolated yourself? Are you vulnerable to the wiles and attacks of the enemy—especially in the area of anxiety?

A Lesson from Geese

Geese fly 73 percent farther together than alone. The *V* formation allows the least amount of wing usage necessary from the geese. Each goose uses the updraft from the one flying in front of him to reduce the amount of energy needed to flap his wings.

Have you ever wondered why geese honk as they fly? Because the lead goose is facing the full force of the headwind. If he dares to look back to see whether his friends are still flying in the proper *V* formation, his neck will suddenly snap.

The geese honk to tell the head goose that they are still rightly structured in their formation and faithfully following him. They haven't left him alone. They are with him and encouraging him to keep flying.

Geese make good teammates.

If one of the geese should get tired, sick, or be shot and fall to the ground, two others from the *V* formation immediately leave to check on their friend. As soon as the fallen goose is able, the three begin flying again—you guessed it—in a *V* formation. It takes at least three geese to reestablish this formation in order to fly 73 percent farther together than alone.

Maybe geese are smarter than humans. Too often we leave our hurting and sick to face life alone. But geese know that they need each other so they can fly farther.

Listen to Your Self-Talk

How can you ascertain whether you are isolated and, as a result, more vulnerable to anxiety?

Listen to your self-talk. All of us have running conversations with ourselves in our mind. What are we saying to ourselves?

If this inner conversation is constantly condemning you, anxiety will increase. If you are speaking words of faith to yourself, you will experience peace.

What are you saying to yourself?

King David knew the importance of positive self-talk. In Psalm 42, he asked, "Why are you cast down, O my soul?" (verse 5). He was questioning why his soul was feeling so much anxiety. He was examining his emotions.

But David didn't stop there. He then said, "Hope in God" (verse 5). This was not a suggestion, but an imperative, a command. *Hope in God!* David was instructing his soul to believe that God was bigger than all his problems.

We should follow his example.

How to Counter Negative Self-Talk

If you are filling your mind with negative self-talk, you need good teammates who can counter what your mind is telling you. They can help correct the false narratives in your mind. With encouraging words, they can replace corrosive doubt with bold faith.

I recall a time when several people started criticizing me with the same negative message. What they said was painful to hear. I have always tried to be a good leader who is willing to listen to criticism. But trying to discern the difference between what is true or false can sometimes be challenging.

I have also believed that if someone calls you a donkey, you shouldn't pay close attention to the opinion. If two people call you a donkey, you should pay more attention to their criticism. But if three people call you a donkey, you may need to buy a saddle.

Three people had called me a donkey. I was ready to buy a saddle…until several of my closest life teammates took me aside and spoke truth to me.

First, they pointed out that these three people had never much liked my ministry. In fact, they didn't much like each other. My friends showed me how critics often seek each other out when they have a unified rallying cry—even when they don't like each other.

I was their common bull's-eye.

Next, my friends wouldn't allow me to believe my accuser's exaggerated lies. They reminded me that my critics didn't really know me. They hadn't spent any time with me. How could they know or judge me?

But my life teammates knew me. They had spent years doing life with me and my family. We had spent countless hours together—both in good times and bad. They told me of how I had influenced their lives for the Lord. They shared with me my positive character qualities. They also reminded me that they wouldn't hesitate to bring concerns to me.

My friends refuted my critics' lies with the truth. And my heart was set free.

This is why we need each other. We need good teammates who will speak words of faith that help overcome our anxieties.

Paul and Barnabas

When Paul began his first missionary journey, he knew the potential perils facing him. Everything from brigands to arrest to torture awaited him. How did he choose to best face these challenging situations?

Paul chose a teammate. He asked Barnabas to accompany him. Barnabas accepted Paul's invitation and remained faithful to Paul throughout his successful first missionary journey.

Barnabas's name means "son of encouragement." His name reveals his character. He was a constant source of positive words for Paul. We can be certain that when Paul became discouraged, Barnabas spoke faith to his mind. Perhaps Barnabas's words helped contribute to the success of Paul's first missionary journey.

Paul may have been thinking about Barnabas when he wrote these words to the Christians at Thessalonica: "Encourage one another and build one another up, just as you are doing" (1 Thessalonians 5:11). Perhaps Paul was saying this because Barnabas had been such a great source of encouragement to him.

Paul may have had Barnabas in mind when he wrote to the Ephesians: "Having put away falsehood, let each one of you speak the truth with his neighbor, for we are members of one another...Let no corrupting talk come out of your mouths, but only such as is good for building up, as fits the occasion, that it may give grace to those who hear" (Ephesians 4:25,29). Perhaps this was the way Barnabas had encouraged Paul.

Positive teammates give life. Negative ones bring discouragement.

We need to use our words to build up one another, not tear each other down, no matter what the situation. We need to give faith to others, not unbelief.

A teammate's words can help us overcome our anxieties.

Jackie Robinson

Jackie Robinson was the first African-American to break the racial barrier in major league baseball. It's well chronicled how difficult this journey was for him. He experienced insufferable indignities and prejudice.

Daily, Robinson tried to persevere. Most of the time he was successful, but one time the pain boiled over and caused Robinson's soul to start withering.

Robinson was on third base during an important game. He had gotten a base hit, stolen second, then advanced to third on an infield out. Hecklers shouted torrents of racial slurs against him from the stands.

Finally, the verbal onslaught was too much to handle. Robinson's insides collapsed. He couldn't take any more. He decided to give up.

That is, until Robinson heard the voice of a young boy yelling to him from the stands. This child's voice pierced through all the others, crying out, "Way to go, Jackie! You are doing great! Keep on! You can do it!"

In that moment, faith overcame fear in Robinson's mind. Encouragement replaced discouragement. Hope overshadowed despair. A new energy invigorated him.

Robinson decided not to give up. One pitch later, he scored the decisive run that gave his team the victory. His teammates slapped him on the back and hugged him. Robinson ran into the dugout with a new resolve to help major league baseball be a place for *all* players of any background or color.

Today, professional baseball has players from many different nations and ethnicities. Their presence is directly attributed to Jackie Robinson's courage and resolve. One game each season, every major league player wears number 42 on his jersey to acknowledge Robinson's contribution to what baseball is today.

And Robinson's success can be connected to a young, unknown fan in the stands yelling positive words in an important game. Robinson was ready to give up. But he persevered. And America is a better and stronger nation because of it.

That young fan was one of Robinson's needed good teammates on his life's journey. This fan replaced Robinson's despair with courage.

We all need such teammates.

Marilynn and Me

I had been in ministry for about 15 years, and challenges had accumulated and taken their toll on me. I had become exhausted, frustrated, depressed, and anxious about my future. I didn't know if I had the strength to continue.

We decided to take a one-week break. We went to a vacation resort, trying desperately to rest. I needed to find out whether my spiritual and emotional batteries could be sufficiently recharged to continue doing ministry. This break was a turning point for me.

The first night away was the hardest. We went to bed at a reasonable hour, thinking a good night's sleep would be my first step toward restoration.

But I couldn't fall asleep. Hour after hour passed with my eyelids propped wide open. I just couldn't fall asleep no matter how hard I tried.

At around three in the morning, Marilynn awakened and sat up in bed. She realized that I'd been awake for hours. She took my hand and didn't say anything for several minutes. Quietly, she finally spoke, "You aren't doing well, are you?"

"No," I responded with a sigh. "I just can't sleep. My thoughts keep focusing on all the problems. They are too heavy on my mind."

Then she said some words that changed everything. Four simple, precise words spoken from her loving lips encouraged my heart and gave me the determination to keep on persevering.

"I believe in you."

That's all she said. *I believe in you.* Four words filled with faith.

Suddenly I knew that I could make it. I could continue to face the obstacles of ministry and overcome them. I was certain that my life's mountains weren't bigger than my God. My faith could and would overcome my fears. I knew that the Jesus who lives in me is greater than the evil one who lives in the world (1 John 4:4).

Today, when a person tells me that he or she has been helped by the ministry God has called me to, I think about that moment at the beach in the early morning hours when Marilynn spoke these four life-giving words to me: "I believe in you." I've never been the same since.

My Marilynn is a good teammate God has given to me in marriage. She spoke encouraging words that changed my trajectory in life and ministry. We all need someone like this—either in our marriage or in a close friendship.

The Paraclete

One of the most remarkable truths of the Christian faith is that when you accept Jesus, the Holy Spirit immediately indwells your heart. He takes up residence inside you. He will never leave you nor forsake you. God's promise of the indwelling Spirit is an eternal promise.

The Greek term translated "Holy Spirit" in the Bible is often *paracletos*. This term is translated in different ways. Literally, it means "the one who walks alongside." He is a partner and friend, a living presence. A life teammate forever.

The *paracletos* is like my Marilynn encouraging me at the beach, only he lives inside us and is with us every single second of every single day.

The Holy Spirit is our greatest encourager.

Another phrase used in the Bible to define the *paracletos* is "the encourager." Think about this definition. God places his living, eternal presence inside us to constantly speak words of life to us in every situation. To make sure that thoughts of faith, not anxiety, continually fill our minds.

The Holy Spirit is our greatest encourager. When the evil one accuses us (Revelation 12:10), we as followers of Jesus need to turn our ear and listen to the voice of the encourager. Scripture explicitly says there is no condemnation for those who are in Christ Jesus (Romans 8:1). None. Condemnation does not come from the encourager. It can't! It comes only from the darkest, hidden crevices of hell.

Yes, God will convict you of your sins. That's one of the works of the Holy Spirit (John 16:8). Yes, he will discipline you for your disobedience in the same way that a loving father chastises a disobedient child. But God does this to change your behavior, not to withdraw his love from you. It's your bad behavior he hates, not you.

The accuser hates you. The encourager loves you. Nothing can ever separate you from God's love—that is a secure promise from his Word (Romans 8:38-39).

Which voice are you listening to? Which one is influencing your emotions?

Make sure that you are hearing the voice of your best teammate—God himself!

My Encouragement Drawer

You may have heard it said that no one has ever erected a statue to a critic. That is true.

It is easy for a critic to find fault with others and tear them down. Conversely, an encourager speaks positive words that build people up—sometimes to the point of giving them new direction and purpose in life.

An easy way to lift someone up is to write a note of encouragement. In fact, I have a drawer in my office desk that is full of almost 40 years of such notes. When I receive one, I add it to the others in my encouragement drawer to be read over repeatedly when I feel discouraged.

I have collected hundreds of these notes through the years. Sometimes I'll dip my hands in the drawer, rummage through the letters, and randomly pick one. Often, it's a note from years before. I'll read the note and feel my faith be built up for days to come.

There are two reasons I bring this up.

First, you can accomplish much good by writing notes to people who need encouragement. Be a good teammate—to your friends facing problems, your pastor dealing with difficult issues, or your family members struggling with life. Find a need someone else is facing and fill it by being a good teammate. Help build their faith so they can overcome their anxieties.

Don't underestimate the power of a note of encouragement. Doing this is easier than ever in an age during which people can communicate through emails and texts. Use any and all mediums available to lift other people up with your words.

Next, save all the encouraging notes you receive from others. The Christmas season provides an especially good opportunity to hoard such notes. But you can receive them from friends and family members all throughout the year. Keep them. Start your own encouragement drawer. And read the notes—especially when you get discouraged.

These notes will lift your heart and give you strength to face the future. You can hold on to them for years and reread them during difficult times. This is a great way to fight worry.

Get New Friends

Several years ago, I was asked to interview will.i.am, the lead singer for the pop music group The Black Eyed Peas. In front of several hundred inner-city youth, I asked him for tips he could share about how to live life well.

It was an enjoyable afternoon with a pop icon. He was funny, engaging, and extremely insightful. He offered wisdom principles to follow. He was so captivating that he had the kids in the palm of his hand.

When our time together came to an end, I asked one final question: "We all know the importance of good teammates to encourage us along life's treacherous roads. First Corinthians 15:33 says that bad company corrupts morals. What would you say to these kids about the importance of having good friends? If they have bad friends leading them down wrong paths, what would you say to them?"

will.i.am paused momentarily. He stroked the hairs on his chin several times, then responded, "I would tell them to get new friends." He said nothing else.

His point was made. His words reminded me of the time my dad compared friends to elevators. They will either take you up or take you down. They will either increase or decrease your faith or your problems. Their words will either build up hope or cause more challenges. You want to find friends who will lift you up.

Both will.i.am and my dad understood the value of positive, encouraging teammates helping us to overcome the problems of life—including our anxieties.

We need one another. Find friends who will build your faith, not increase your worry.

Trials Help Identify Your Positive Teammates

Reflecting on four decades of ministry, Marilynn and I have come to realize that this kind of work is not for the fainthearted. Different sorts of trials and tribulations await those called to do the Lord's work. Every one will prove a challenge.

However, one especially difficult situation stands out above all others. There was a time when we faced subterfuge and betrayal. People whom we had thought were our friends turned out to be enemies.

Eventually Marilynn and I were able to walk through the situation with our heads held high. We can now see how God used these painful fires to further forge our faith. As a result, we came into a deeper relationship with Jesus. Our great marriage became even greater as we pressed into one another like never before. We lamented the past but learned how to look ahead to a future filled with hope. We learned to give thanks in all things, even this situation, because God was using it for good.

One special way that the Lord used the situation for good was to enable us to identify the people who were our true teammates. Casual friends never contacted us. Those on the periphery of our lives were nowhere to be found.

Our real teammates and friends called us frequently to give us encouraging words. They sent texts daily. They checked on us regularly. They invited us to dinner. They built our faith and reduced our fears.

> **Tough times reveal who your true teammates are.**

These good teammates were always present in some way or other. Sometimes they didn't say a word when they were with us. They just sat there and let us emote as we needed to. Those may have been our richest times together. Their presence expressed deep love and cemented our friendship. We couldn't have made it through this hard time without them.

Tough times reveal who your true teammates are. They expose faux friends and confirm real relationships. This is one reason we can rejoice in our trials (Romans 5:3).

Don't ever underestimate the need for good teammates to help build up your faith. They are an important part of walking through life's journey successfully.

Final Thoughts

Monitor your self-talk. What are you saying to yourself? Make sure you become a good friend to *you*. Just as Jesus tells you how much he loves and accepts you, tell yourself that you are loved and valued. Refuse to allow your soul to become downcast. Constantly command yourself to place your hope in God. Always remember that you need to be a good teammate to yourself.

Listen to the voice of the Holy Spirit in you, not the accuser. The Holy

Spirit will always enlarge your faith and encourage you. The accuser's goal is to diminish your faith and discourage you. The Holy Spirit will convict you of your wrong behavior, yet always remain faithful to you. The accuser will tell you that you could never be loved by God because of all your sins.

Which of these two options is going to give you peace, security, and acceptance? The answer is obvious. The Holy Spirit is a good teammate. Listen to him.

Start an encouragement drawer. Set aside all the positive notes you receive. Pull them out regularly to read and reread them. Your heart will be lifted with hope when you do this. As you read your notes, your teammates will speak to you once again.

By the way, I have a few notes of encouragement written to me by my dad before he died. I read them again and again. In this way, he still speaks words of life and faith to me—he does this from heaven. How special is that?

Choose your friends wisely. If they are pulling you down and discouraging you, get new friends. If you're around negative people, they will destroy your life and exacerbate your anxieties. Surround yourself with people who love to see you chase your dreams and succeed—with those who will build up your faith, not tear it down.

Life is a team sport. You need positive people around you. Good teammates will help you fight your fears, not give in to them.

Get good teammates.

And watch anxiety lose its destructive grip on your heart.

CHAPTER 14

REALIZE GOD DID NOT GIVE YOU A SPIRIT OF FEAR

Fear does not come from God (2 Timothy 1:7). Rather, he wants his people to enjoy lives free of fear and full of peace. Jesus came to give us life abundantly (John 10:10). Power, love, and self-control should describe the life of a believer, not fear.

Jesus didn't walk in fear. And if his life abides in us, why are we walking in fear? If we are connected to Jesus as a branch is to a vine, anxiety must be replaced with faith (John 15:5). Jesus did only the will of his Father, and so should we (John 6:38). He is in us, and we are in him. When we are rightly connected to Jesus, fear should flee from our hearts.

What else should Jesus's followers know to combat anxiety and fear and live in complete victory and freedom?

Dealing with the Spirit of Fear

The Greek word translated "fear" in 2 Timothy 1:7 refers to someone who flees from a battle. It suggests cowardice and timidity. It describes a victim, not a victor.

Biblically, when one is walking close to God, boldness should consume the heart. "The wicked flee when no one pursues, but the righteous are bold as a lion" (Proverbs 28:1). God promised the Israelites that when he was present, one of them would cause 1,000 to flee (Deuteronomy 32:30).

Followers of Jesus have no reason to possess a spirit of fear.

What does the phrase "spirit of fear" mean (2 Timothy 1:7 NKJV)? Several suggestions have been given by scholars. It could refer to the Holy Spirit in the hearts of believers who possess no fear. His presence should drive out all fear and enable us to bear his fruit (Galatians 5:22-23).

Some suggest the word "spirit," *pneuma* in the Greek text, can be translated "attitude." That is, God never gives his people an attitude of fear. Fear should never consume the believer's thought life. Rather, the Christian's mind should be marked by an attitude of faith. That point has been made throughout this book.

Or the "spirit of fear" could be referring to demonic agencies or spiritual foes who want to destroy people. They are the demonic hordes who possessed and oppressed people in Jesus's day. They are still at work today.

Some Christians connect this "spirit of fear" to what Paul was warning Christians about in Ephesians 6:12—that we are not warring against flesh and blood, but against the powers and principalities of the darkness.

These demons, overseen by the evil one, hate those of us who are followers of Jesus. They work tirelessly to discourage and thwart us—especially God's purpose for us. And two of their chief weapons are fear and anxiety. That's why Christians must be ready to do spiritual warfare.

Up till now, we've looked at 11 ways to fight anxiety.

This final way, which has to do with spiritual warfare, is equally important, if not more so. As someone once said, you can't fight a rattlesnake with a squirt gun. Nor can you fight a spiritual enemy with carnal weapons. More is needed; God's power must be used.

Understanding Demonic Influence

Can a committed Christian be possessed by demonic spirits? Of course not. If someone is filled with the Holy Spirit, it is impossible for a demon to dwell in that person. Filled means *filled*! There is no room for anything except the fullness of Jesus.

That's why it's important for Christians to be filled with the Holy Spirit (Ephesians 5:18)—that is, to be fully yielded to him who dwells in us. We are not to be under the influence of anything earthly, such as alcohol. We are to be fully led, influenced, and controlled by the Holy Spirit who lives in us.

The Greek verb translated "filled" in Ephesians 5:18 is in the imperfect tense. It refers to a continual, daily, regular infilling. It suggests that as we serve Jesus, there is an emptying of him in us to a dying world. That's why we need regular, daily infillings. As a car runs out of gas, so can we be emptied of the Holy Spirit's presence and power.

Christians need daily times with Jesus, times that are filled with prayer and God's Word. We need regular encounters with the Spirit's love, grace, gifts, and fruit. It's imperative we make this a habit.

And if we don't? We can open our hearts to demonic influence. The evil one and his enemy hordes will look for every portal that gives them an opportunity to attack. As a coach spends countless hours studying game films to exploit an opponent's weaknesses, so does the enemy of our souls try to find every possible vulnerability in us.

If Christians focus on the mountains rather than the Creator of the mountain, the enemy will send a spirit of fear to attack. If we stare at the problem and not God's possibilities, the enemy will summon a spirit of fear to attack. If we continually look at the mess instead of the One who controls all, the enemy will call upon a spirit of fear to attack.

The evil one wants to cripple our faith. He does not want us to walk in victory over him. That's why he is eager to bring anxiety into our lives. Author David Platt said it well: "We become what we behold. The more we focus on Christ, the more he will be reflected in our lives."[17]

We will eventually become whatever we focus on in our thought life. And the enemy is ready to pounce when he sees us looking at life's difficulties instead of God himself.

Realizing God Is Sovereign

The enemy and his demonic army are relentless. They want to destroy us; that is their passion.

But please don't become overly discouraged about that. Instead, remember this truth: The evil one is a creature. God is the Creator. The enemy is under God's sovereignty. He can't do anything to you unless the Father in heaven allows it.

Numerous examples of this truth are found in the Bible.

Jesus and Peter

Jesus predicted that Peter would be disloyal to him (Luke 22:31-34). Peter objected and proudly proclaimed that he would never desert Jesus. He loved him too much. His devotion was undeniable. He had left everything to follow the Lord. He was even willing to go to prison and die for Jesus.

Jesus informed Peter that Satan had demanded to sift him like wheat. The enemy would prompt Peter to panic to the point of denying that he even knew Jesus.

Jesus granted permission for Satan to carry out this attack.

And that's exactly what happened—Peter denied that he knew Jesus. Not once, or even twice, but three times. He betrayed the beloved. During Jesus's agonizing, horrifically painful six hours on the cross, Peter was nowhere to be found. He had run away. Fled in fear. A coward to the core.

Because Jesus is the sovereign Lord of the universe, he knew this would happen. He also knew that later, he would forgive Peter for his betrayal and restore their relationship.

Knowing the Father's perfect plan, Jesus told Peter that after Satan had sifted him, his faith would increase. It would become secure like never before.

In other words, Jesus let Peter know that Satan was on a leash. Yes, he is a formidable foe, but one overseen by the Creator. Satan was being used by Jesus to grow Peter's faith.

Could God be permitting the evil one to attack you to show you the chinks in your spiritual armor? Is he permitting the enemy to use anxiety to sift you like wheat so that he can show you a place where your faith needs to grow?

One way an athlete gets better is by entering a competition and losing. When he is pummeled, he discovers his weaknesses. Isn't it interesting that the event athletes must attend to try out for their nation's Olympic team is called the Olympic Trials? You can't make the team unless you go through the trials.

For this reason, you can give thanks to God for your anxiety. In this way, you can discover the weak points in your faith—weak points that must be addressed so you can be conformed to the image of Jesus and used by him for ministry. Anxiety can show where unbelief is present and your faith is weak.

> **God is using *all* things, even the enemy,
> in our lives for our good and his glory.**

God may be using spiritual assaults and a spirit of fear to deepen your life in him. To show you places where your life isn't completely hidden in Jesus (Colossians 3:3). To give you insights into areas where you aren't finding rest for your soul (Matthew 11:29).

Always remember that the devil is the devil. He *is* powerful. But he is subject to God. And God is using *all* things, even the enemy, in our lives for our good and his glory (Romans 8:28). The word "all" in that passage includes anxiety.

Anxiety reveals to us our need to develop more trust in the One who died on the cross and was raised from the dead to give his eternal love to us.

A Lying Spirit

King Ahab was a debauched ruler over Israel's northern kingdom. He introduced pagan idolatry and religious syncretism to God's people. He was one of the Bible's worst kings.

Facing a common foe, Ahab tried to convince King Jehoshaphat, a good king in Israel's southern kingdom, to join him in battle. Jehoshaphat hesitated before making this commitment. He asked for counsel from some prophets before deciding what to do.

Several godless prophets from Ahab's court appeared before the two kings. They enthusiastically exhorted the two kings to form an alliance and enter the battle together. They were confident that the battle would be easily won.

Jehoshaphat wasn't so sure of the prophets' confidence. Something just didn't seem right. Perhaps he wondered if the prophets were simply telling Ahab what he wanted to hear. They may have been afraid to say anything negative to Ahab.

Jehoshaphat wanted a second opinion. He demanded that Ahab send for Micaiah, a prophet known for pulling no punches. Truth-telling was his highest priority, and he didn't care whom he was speaking to. He feared God alone. Pleasing people was not a part of his nature.

Now it was Ahab's turn to be hesitant. He sighed and complained that Micaiah spoke only negative news. Ahab had never heard anything positive from Micaiah's lips. That only made Jehoshaphat want to hear more from Micaiah.

The kings sent for Micaiah. Surprisingly, his first words to Ahab were exactly those of the other prophets. But Ahab saw that his words were not what they appeared to be on the surface. They were mocking imitations of what the false prophets had said.

Then Micaiah spoke the truth. He saw a vision of God holding court in heaven. It was a council of war, with God sitting on his throne. He was surrounded by his army, and they were making plans on how to defeat Ahab in battle.

In the invisible world, God was ready to influence what was going to happen in the visible world. Though God himself can never do evil, he sometimes orders evil agents to accomplish his purposes. God allowed a lying spirit to go to Ahab and cause him to believe that he would win the battle (1 Kings 22:22).

This is similar to when God allowed a "harmful spirit" to torment King Saul. He was losing his power to David as king. This harmful spirit was a form of judgment from God upon Saul to accomplish his purposes and raise up David as the next king (1 Samuel 16:14).

The lying spirit left heaven, came to earth, and convinced Ahab of victory. The king proudly marched into battle, yet he lost not only the battle, but his life (1 Kings 22:34-35).

How are we to understand what happened here? God sovereignly oversees everything, including lying and harmful spirits. He can use them as he wills and for his purposes. A lying spirit helped convince Ahab about what he wanted to do.

Notice that God was the one controlling the lying spirit's work. This spirit only did what God wanted him to do.

Could God be permitting a spirit of fear to reveal something to you? Could he be allowing it to attack you so that you can realize that faith does not reign supreme in your life? Is God revealing vulnerable weaknesses you have not allowed him to control?

Joseph and His Brothers

Joseph's brothers planned his demise. They threw him into a pit, sold him to traders in a caravan going to Egypt, and told their grief-stricken dad that he was dead. Though the text does not tell us that the enemy was behind all this, it surely smells of his work.

Years later, after Joseph was raised up by God to become Egypt's prime minister, his brothers came to Egypt during a famine, desperate for food. They came into Joseph's presence, not knowing who he was, requesting relief. But Joseph knew who they were.

When Joseph finally revealed his identity to his brothers, they begged for mercy. They thought their lives were finished. They were sure that karma would turn against them and they would be killed.

Astonishingly, Joseph forgave them. Then he stated, "You meant evil against me, but God meant it for good" (Genesis 50:20).

When Joseph was sold into slavery then ended up in jail, all looked hopeless. But God oversaw all the enemy's actions and used them for good. He providentially knew that a famine was coming upon the land. He was also aware that by making Joseph the prime minister of Egypt, the Jewish people would have a way of surviving the famine.

The Jews needed to continue to exist so Jesus could later enter human history and die for the sins of the world. Unless Joseph had been sent to Egypt by God, there would not have been someone in a position to preserve them so they could return to the Promised Land, the place where Jesus would be born in Bethlehem—as the prophet Micah foretold (Micah 5:2).

God used evil for good. He always does this for his children.

What good might God be trying to show you in the midst of your anxiety? If you were able to eliminate the anxiety in your life, what good could you do for the advancement of God's kingdom?

Job

Job's trials are well documented. He lost almost everything he had. His children were killed. His earthly wealth was decimated. His physical health deteriorated. His life was in ruins. And his wife begged him to curse God, thinking perhaps this would somehow alleviate the suffering.

But cursing God was the one thing Job could not do. He refused. However, like a beaten puppy, he did whimper about the extremely difficult circumstances he faced.

That was the picture of Job on the earthly stage. However, behind the scenes in the heavenly realm, another part of the story had been unfolding. The enemy first had to ask God for permission to sift Job like wheat.

God gave the evil one permission to touch everything that Job owned except one thing: his life. The right to life and death rested solely in God's sovereign hand.

Once the evil one was given permission by God, he attacked Job viciously. Thus the horrific destruction we see presented in the first chapter of Job.

Three friends came to comfort Job. But through their words, they only added to his agony. They pontificated about potential sins Job had committed, assuming that disobedience was the reason for God's punishment of him.

What was God doing with Job? Scholars throughout the centuries have offered different perspectives.

Personally, I've come to believe that God was dealing with Job's pride and self-righteousness. Though Job was a righteous man in many ways, like so many of us (including me!), pride lurked under the surface of his heart. It's a deadly, stealthy disease that goes unnoticed. Pride is what caused the devil to rebel against God and become the enemy. Pride is antithetical to faith.

If so, that means God loved Job enough to allow the enemy to attack and deal with an evil keeping him from the fullness of faith and righteousness. In fact, Job didn't get relief until two things happened.

First, Job recognized God's sovereignty. He realized that God, not he, created everything in the world (chapters 38–42). He understood that all is a gift from God to be richly enjoyed. Recognizing God's complete rule over all is the optimal way to defeat pride. When we do this, we pray, "Who am I, Lord, that you give me a glancing thought? I am nothing. Jesus is everything."

Next, God adjured Job to forgive his three friends for their careless, thoughtless interactions with him. The fruit of pride is bitterness. Perhaps God was using Job's bitterness toward his friends to reveal to him an ugly area of self-righteousness.

When bitterness invades a human heart, it is like a marauding army. Bitterness destroys and defiles everything in its path (Hebrews 12:15). Intimacy with Jesus is diminished. He cannot fill a heart with faith and love when it is filled with resentment.

Job forgave his friends (Job 42:10). He blessed them as God instructed him. He set them free to let God take vengeance on them. That was God's job, not Job's (see Romans 12:19).

Through all he endured, Job was forced to deal with his pride. And bitterness was jettisoned from his soul. He was set free to enjoy life anew.

Afterward, God restored twofold all that had been taken from Job (Job 42:10). Notice that the Lord didn't just restore what was lost; he gave Job double for all the trouble he had faced.

This isn't the only time in Scripture that we see God giving a double portion. While the people of the southern kingdom of Israel were held captive in Babylon for 70 years, God promised a future and a hope for them (Jeremiah 29:11). He also covenanted to return them to the Promised Land with a double restoration for all their woes (Isaiah 61:7; Zechariah 9:12).

That is what happened with Job. He lost everything, and God restored it double.

But first, pride and self-righteousness had to be dealt with. Forgiveness had to replace bitterness. Then and only then did the blessing occur. The double restoration came after Job humbled himself and forgave his tormenters.

> **Your fiery trials won't last forever. But they won't be over until God's work is accomplished.**

There is purpose in your pain. God is using it for his plans. He is using the enemy's wiles, schemes, and destruction against you for your good.

Your fiery trials won't last forever. But they won't be over until God's work is accomplished.

That's because God *is* good. And he is sovereign over all.

What does the Lord want to teach you in your difficult times? Is pride present in your life? Self-righteousness? Unbelief? Bitterness? Strife? Resentment? What is the source of your anxiety? Once you identify what God wants to deal with, you can confess it, take steps to eliminate it, and go on to enjoy a richer life in Jesus.

Yes, the enemy is a roaring lion, prowling around the earth looking for someone to destroy (1 Peter 5:7). Yes, he is trying to discover weaknesses in your life so that he can exploit and hurt you. He is an evil destroyer.

Yet God is able to use the enemy for his divine purposes. As a result, our faith and trust will grow and deepen.

The evil one doesn't like it when believers trust Jesus more and more. He despises simple, childlike faith. He doesn't want us to look constantly to our heavenly home. He hates when we realize that all afflictions here are light and momentary when compared to eternity's bliss (2 Corinthians 4:17). He doesn't want us to set our minds on things above (Colossians 3:2).

Instead, the enemy wants us to become proud and bitter. Then our faith will wither.

And anxiety will increase.

Responding by Ministering the Opposite

Some Bible interpreters believe there is evidence that different kinds of spirits afflict humans. Here are a few of them.

The spirit of Jezebel is seen in Revelation in the church at Thyatira (Revelation 2:18-29). This spirit was present in King Ahab's wife. Though genderless, this is a controlling spirit that leads to rebellion and witchcraft.

The spirit of Leviathan is a slithery, multiheaded monster mentioned in several different places in the Bible. It operates in secret, under murky waters, and is motivated by pride. This spirit is a strong principality and wants to bring down ministries and divide the church.

The spirit of Absalom wants to overthrow people who are in power. David's son Absalom led a rebellion against his father. This spirit is motivated primarily by bitter jealousy and selfish ambition (James 3:13-16). It divides and devours people. It is earthly, unspiritual, and demonic.

The spirit of fear was mentioned by Paul to his protégé, Timothy, in 2 Timothy 1:7. This spirit is not from God and causes cowardice and timidity. God wants his people to have love, peace, and a sound mind that is singularly focused on him. God yearns for our minds to be controlled by faith, not fear.

If any of these spirits are operative in your world, here is wise counsel: Minister the opposite. Find the opposite of these spirits and confront them. Live out humility, forgiveness, truth, and faith. These spirits cannot stand to be in the presence of someone living fully in God's grace and glory.

For example, if you feel like someone in your life has the controlling spirit of Jezebel, remove yourself from his or her presence. That person will become infuriated when he or she can't control you. But it's your choice whether to stay in the friendship or not. Remove yourself, and the power of the Jezebel spirit will be broken.

If someone in your life has the Leviathan spirit, minister humility. Practice personal confession. Refuse bitterness. Walk humbly with your God. Those who have the Leviathan spirit are mad when you choose to respond with humility.

If someone has a lying spirit, minister truth. Humbly speak the truth in love (Ephesians 4:15). Make sure love saturates your words. Otherwise, you will only increase the strife, and that's the desire of the lying spirit. Jesus is the way, the truth, and the life (John 14:6). He said that when we abide in his Word, we will know the truth, and the truth will set us free (John 8:31-32).

Lying spirits hate the bright light of truth. When we speak the truth, they leave.

If you suspect a spirit of fear has invaded your heart, minister the opposite. Feed your heart with faith. Seek first God's kingdom (Matthew 6:33). Memorize God's Word and speak faith-filled verses to your mind all day long. Concentrate on what is good, honorable, pure, and just (Philippians 4:8). Refuse to let a fearful thought enter your mind.

Inform your thought life with what may be the two most important words in the Bible: *But God.* When the enemy and his destructive hordes speak anxious words to you, respond by saying, "But God." God is God; the enemy is not. God is all-powerful and omniscient; the enemy is not.

Repeat this prayer throughout your day:

> I don't care what I see. I don't walk by sight, but by faith. I refuse to pay attention to the enemy's lies. I know that my Redeemer lives. And I have the faith to cling to the Lord's promises no matter what. Heaven is my home. If I don't get to experience God's promises until then, so be it. God has his reasons for waiting. But God. His delay doesn't mean he is denying me. I trust him. Like a child, I believe. And that's that!

That kind of prayer drives the enemy and his hordes crazy. It reminds him that he is a creature, not the Creator, and thus he is not sovereign. It reminds him of his coming eternal doom, and how each passing day draws him closer to hell. And you to heaven.

Your prayer of faith will conquer the enemy's wiles. He will realize yet again that he may be the devil, but God is still in control. And God is using the devil's attacks for his purposes. And our good.

Praise God, Jesus is Lord!

Final Thoughts

Until Jesus returns and sets up his kingdom, the evil one and his fallen angels will continue to try to wreak havoc on God's created order. They will try to destroy and divide God's people. Satan's craft and wiles are great; he is armed with cruel hate. On earth is not his equal.

But God—he is on our side (Psalm 118:13). Remember, you plus God is a majority. We should celebrate those odds!

Like Elisha, we should ask God to peel back the veil that separates this world from the next and let us see that there are *so* many powerful angels, in chariots of fire, fighting for us (2 Kings 6:17). God is for us (Romans 8:31). Thanks be to God that we have won the victory with Jesus (2 Corinthians 2:14)!

Trust God in your trials. If you are under demonic assault right now, ask God for his angels to help you. Believe that the angel of the Lord is not only defeating your enemy but pursuing him (Psalm 35:5-6). This is the victory that overcomes the world: your *faith* (1 John 5:4).

Believe. Trust. Surrender all to your heavenly Daddy who loves you so much.

And anxiety will flee.

EVERYTHING YOU NEED TO OVERCOME ANXIETY

The Bible repeatedly admonishes Christians not to worry about anything. Fear is not from God. Worry should not be a part of our lives.

Don't you want to live beyond anxiety? Don't you desire to be free from its assaults upon your soul, and for it to go away?

If anxiety isn't from God, he will surely give you the resources you need to become more than a conqueror. You *can* do all things through Christ, who gives you the strength to face troublesome and impossible situations.

Think about this: God wants you to live free from anxiety even more than you do. How deep is the Father's love for you!

The Bible is filled with reminders and promises that God *will* take care of you and that you *can* know peace when life is difficult. You *can* experience his love when all seems hopeless. It is powerfully reassuring to review God's words of comfort and help when they are put together:

> Do not be anxious about anything, but in everything by prayer and supplication, with thanksgiving let your requests be known to God (Philippians 4:6).

> Peace I leave with you; my peace I give to you. Not as the world gives do I give to you. Let not your hearts be troubled, neither let them be afraid (John 14:27).

> Fear not, for I am with you; be not dismayed, for I am your

God; I will strengthen you, I will help you, I will uphold you with my righteous right hand (Isaiah 41:10).

When the cares of my heart are many, your consolations cheer my soul (Psalm 94:19).

I sought the Lord, and he answered me and delivered me from all my fears (Psalm 34:4).

Cast all your anxiety on him because he cares for you (1 Peter 5:7 niv).

I tell you, do not be anxious about your life, what you will eat, nor about your body, what you will put on (Luke 12:22).

God has not given us a spirit of fear, but of power and of love and of a sound mind (2 Timothy 2:17 nkjv).

You keep him in perfect peace whose mind is stayed on you, because he trusts in you (Isaiah 26:3).

Come to me, all who labor and are heavy laden, and I will give you rest (Matthew 11:28).

There is no fear in love, but perfect love drives out fear. For fear has to do with punishment, and whoever fears has not been perfected in love (1 John 4:18).

Say to those who have an anxious heart, "Be strong; fear not! Behold, your God will come with vengeance, with the recompense of God. He will come and save you" (Isaiah 35:4).

Let not your hearts be troubled. Believe in God; believe also in me (John 14:1).

As you've seen all throughout this book, you don't have to live in anxiety. There are cures. God has provided the means for you to achieve victory. We've looked at 12 practical ways to confront and conquer anxiety, and these are methods that Jesus's followers have used for centuries:

1. *Focus on faith*. Believe. Biblically, faith is always the antidote to anxiety. Anxious thoughts reveal areas of your life not yet totally surrendered to Jesus. His love will overwhelm those places of anxiety as you trust in Jesus.

2. *Pray*. God has given you prayer as a means of communicating your anxious thoughts to him. Give them all to the Lord. Refuse to carry them any longer. Let him do that. His love is stronger than your worry. Perfect love *does* cast out all fear.

3. *Fast*. Fast from anything that is keeping your life from true intimacy with Jesus. It could be food, drink, social media, or something else. Deny yourself that earthly idol and completely depend on the One who created you. How much he loves you!

4. *Cast*. Cast *all* your cares upon Jesus because he cares for you. When you doubt God's care, remember the cradle. He left heaven to pursue you in love. Remember the cross. He died for you to forgive you of your sins. Are there any two greater acts of love?

5. *Consider creation*. Look at the beauty and majesty of the creation that surrounds you. If God designed this world with such great care, that means he designed you with great care as well. You can trust the God of creation with your anxieties. He created you to be a container of his love.

6. *Ponder the prepositions*. God is *with* you. He desires his love to live *in* you. He goes *before* you. He exists *over* you, controlling all. He is *around* you, encouraging you to keep moving forward toward life's finish line. He lives *through* you. You are his hands and feet in the world. If all these things are true, why be anxious about anything?

7. *Remember*. Recollect the biblical accounts of the parting of the Red Sea and the resurrection. Remember the miracles God has done in your own past. If God came through before, he can do it again! Trust him with your anxieties. His love is evident in your life.

8. *Sing.* God loves music. He invented it. Our insides are lifted up when we sing. If you feel anxious, sing! Do so with others—especially in worship. Studies show that singing produces positive emotions. And is there a more positive emotion in the world than God's love?

9. *Remember your body.* You are body, soul, and spirit—these elements of your humanity are thoroughly interconnected. Your emotions can affect what is happening to your body. Make sure you exercise regularly, sleep enough hours, eat well, and drink lots of water. The God who made your body deeply loves your emotions as well.

10. *Develop an eternal perspective.* No matter what you are feeling, God is still on his throne. He is overseeing all. Let him run his world. Your anxiety will diminish when you do. He is sovereign over everything on this side of eternity and cares for you with his eternal, perfect love.

11. *Get good teammates.* Live your life with people who will build up your faith, not tear it down. Find people who speak positive words to you, not negative ones. Negative people can create anxiety in your life. Don't let them influence you. Allow God's love to motivate you.

12. *Realize that God did not give you a spirit of fear.* His will for you is love, peace, and a sound mind. Your anxiety may be spiritual in nature. Fight the enemy with faith. Realize anew that God loves you so much that he was willing to die on a cross to have a relationship with you. And watch the enemy flee.

May God's grace guide you and give you victory over anxiety. May you now move *beyond* anxiety—for this is God's will for your life.

In Jesus's mighty name, I pray this for you.

FAITH IS MORE OFTEN CAUGHT THAN TAUGHT

When parents try to address the problem of anxiety in their children, it is important for them to realize how much they may end up contributing to anxiety in their children's lives. If you are anxious, you can expect your children to be anxious. If you are worrying about most everything, you can expect your children to worry as well.

Faith is more often caught than taught. You can tell your children repeatedly not to worry or be fearful. But if they see you being worried and fearful, they will do the same. The example you set for your children is undeniable.

Moses understood this problem. He wrote that the sins of the fathers are passed on to the third and fourth generations (Deuteronomy 5:9). When reading these verses, some Bible interpreters have suggested that sin is passed on through a spiritual curse from one generation to another because of a parent's disobedience to God. They compare this to how genetic predispositions are passed on.

For example, when you visit a doctor, he or she will ask you questions about your family history. Is there any incident of heart disease? Or diabetes? Or arthritis? Or cancer? Or dementia? In the same way, some theologians believe spiritual predispositions can be passed along to younger generations.

That raises some difficult questions: Can a child be held responsible for a parent's rebellious decisions? Will a child inherit a spiritual curse from a disobedient parent? If so, how does that work? How could a loving Father in heaven curse a child for the sins of his earthly father?

Essentially, Deuteronomy 5 is addressing the reality of how four different generations within a similar family system can all know and influence one another.

For example, in my wife's present family lineage, her dad is still alive, then there are Marilynn and me, followed by our three kids, and then all our grandkids. Our grandkids know their great-grandad, or Marilynn's dad. Their lives intersect. They have observed his life and heard his stories of courage and valor from World War II. They ask him questions and learn from his wisdom. They have seen how he cares for his invalid wife. That's four generations of familial and relational interaction. Great-grandchildren learning from their great-grandad, and more.

Now connect the dots. If Marilynn's dad were a worrier (which he is not), Marilynn could have assimilated his worrisome nature. Then her worry could have been lived out in our home and passed on to our children, who in turn could have passed fear on to their children.

If that had happened, then Marilynn's dad would have passed on the curse of his worry to the third and fourth generations, just as Moses stated.

That's the bad news. But here is the good news: The curse is not irreversible. It can be broken by one parent becoming a follower of Jesus. When a parent becomes a Christian and surrenders everything to Jesus, he removes all fear from his life and gives his children an example of how to live by faith, without worries.

A follower of Jesus lets faith rule his heart. Faith then causes fear to flee. The curse of fear is reversed. It has no more power over him and his family. The curse is forever eliminated from his life and the lives of his kids. And children who are raised in faith-filled homes live in the covenant promises of the Lord to the *thousandth* generation (Deuteronomy 7:9).

Think about that! The curse of worry can be passed down to the third and fourth generations. But the blessing of faith through God's grace can be handed off to the *thousandth* generation. Which option sounds better to you? Fairly obvious, isn't it?

Keys to Raising Anxiety-Free Children

More specifically, what can you do as a parent to prevent anxiety from taking hold in the hearts of your children? Here are two suggestions:

Walk by Faith

Children today are struggling with anxiety like never before. Why is this happening? I recently read an article by Megan McArdle in the *Washington Post*.[18] I do not know her faith perspective, but the insights she gave in the article were intriguing.

She began by quoting from an essay written in 1827 by English author William Hazlitt. It was titled, "On the Feeling of Immortality in Youth." Again, note the year: 1827, which is almost 200 years ago. He wrote that "no young man believes he shall ever die…to be young is to be as one of the immortal gods."

How true that is! Most young people think that they are invincible. Nothing can knock them down and keep them down. Most cultures would affirm that their youth seem to have had an antianxiety contagion injected into them. They are fearless and act as if nothing can overcome them.

McArdle then said, "Except maybe the current one." She was talking about our present generation of youth.

McArdle then referenced a book written by Greg Lukianoff and Jonathan Haidt, which has the fascinating title *The Coddling of the American Mind*. The authors suggested that contemporary young people "tend to be obsessed with safety, troubled by a pervasive sense of threat. Consequently, understandably, they're anxious and depressed." Did you catch those last few words? Young people today are anxious and depressed like never before.

What happened? How did this present generation become so fearful? What prompted this onslaught of anxiety?

McArdle analyzed phenomena that have exacerbated anxiety among youth. First, she pointed to school shootings. They are indeed unimaginably wicked. But she also pointed out how they are very rare. They don't happen that often.

She points out that there are approximately 55 million school-aged kids in the United States. On average, about ten of them are killed annually at a school.

Don't misunderstand—I am *not* diminishing the fact some children have lost their lives. That statistic is ten too many kids lost annually to school shootings. But be aware that this percentage hasn't changed since the 1990s. In fact, *all* school shootings are listed in that number, not only mass shootings.

Some readers might not like this perspective. How about this: Comparatively speaking, when kids do die today, it's much more often because of suicide. Or a car crash. Or a drug overdose. It seems a disproportionate amount of attention is paid to school shootings when there are other greater dangers faced by children—dangers too often overlooked.

Again, comparatively speaking, today's children are safer with many legal and commonsense protective steps taken by the government and by families to care for them. For example, they receive constant information about eating well and the need for better nutrition. Automobiles are full of all kinds of warning systems and safety devices. Security systems are more advanced than ever before.

Which begs the question: Why is there so much worry in our children today?

McArdle surmised that the news media must share some of the blame. School shootings and kidnappings immediately go national. They capture the headlines for several days. While these events *are* rare, everyone wants to read about them. Whatever the media handles in a sensational manner is going to grab everyone's attention. Sad to say, headline writers know that if it bleeds, it leads. Shocking news is read news.

When people see a jarring headline, fear kicks in. Parents immediately try to process how to protect their kids and all other loved ones in their sphere of influence. They become fearful themselves and put their kids on an instant fear alert.

From there, the parents' worry consumes their hearts and grows. Anxiety begets anxiety. It's a nasty, rapidly expanding contagion.

Perhaps it's time for us as parents to step to the plate and accept some of the responsibility for our kids' anxieties. Our worry is likely increasing their worry. Maybe we are a major reason why anxiety has become epidemic among our children.

Yes, we as parents should make our children aware of dangers. But have we gone over the top? Have we become so overworried that we end up creating a higher level of worry in our offspring?

Remember: Faith is more often caught than taught. The same is true with anxiety.

These are important questions that parents should have the courage to ask themselves. If we are creating fear in our kids' lives, we need to repent. Ask God for forgiveness. And change our own worry-filled behavior.

It's imperative for us as parents to pass faith, not fear, on to our kids. They *must* see a vibrant, living faith consume our hearts before we can hope to calm theirs.

> **Our children will follow our example much more than they will follow our words.**

Let your kids see your faith. Show them that your faith is not mere words but vital action. Allow them to see that you are trusting God in every area of your life. This is essential for helpings kids to see how they can overcome anxiety.

Our children will follow our example much more than they will follow our words.

Is your faith real, vibrant, and alive? In which way are you influencing your children more—through your faith, or through your worries?

Teach Your Kids to Persevere

One of the most important lessons my dad taught me was to never give up. While I was growing up, he warned me repeatedly that in this life we will have tribulations (see John 16:33). He said that everyone, no matter who they are, will face difficult trials. That's a fact of life.

Dad knew that when I got knocked down, I needed to learn to get back up again. He told me over and over that I was a failure only if I never tried again.

Dad reminded me of Romans 5:3-5. He said that I needed to learn how to rejoice in my tribulations, to thank God for trials. Why? Dad knew that problems are God's way of teaching perseverance. He understood that I would learn valuable lessons by facing and battling through my problems.

Dad told me that once I had passed through the trial and arrived on the other side, I would have proven character. *Proven* character. That means character that has been put to the test, that has gone through the fire and come out stronger. He said that I would then know a new depth of God's love, a grace poured into my soul by the power of the Holy Spirit.

Dad's teaching became real to me during one of my high school basketball games. In that game, I played so poorly that I cost my team a needed victory. Not only did I play bad, but I missed the free throws down the stretch that could have won the game.

Dejected, I came home and sought Dad's counsel. I needed a shoulder to cry on. Instead, he gave me a lecture. He wouldn't give in to my victimization. He sat up in his chair and pointedly asked me, "Well, son, what did you learn from losing?"

That's *not* what I wanted to hear. I wanted empathy. Instead, I received what I considered to be a silly question.

Defensively, I tried to manipulate the situation. I went back to my pain and disappointment.

But Dad refused to let me go there. He would have none of it. He didn't allow me to nurse my pain. Rather, he wanted to know what I had gleaned from the failure.

Slowly, I began to offer possibilities for how this situation could be used for good. I needed to work on my free throws and learn how to play under pressure. I had to get myself in better physical shape so I wouldn't be so tired at the end of the game—the time when fatigue makes cowards of players. I needed to know how to play without anxiety and fear of failure.

Dad looked at me and smiled. "There you go. That's my boy! Now you're growing and learning!" he exclaimed. "That's how you must handle life. Learn from your failures. Keep moving forward. Don't be a victim. That attitude will kill you in life. And try to avoid repeating what caused your failure. I'm proud of you! If you learn these lessons, it's good that you have failed."

That was a life moment I'll never forget.

Later, my college basketball coach taught me to handle failure in a similar way. First, admit it. Own up to the mistake. Make it yours. Don't blame others for your failure or be the victim. Next, quit it. Learn from your mistake. Don't repeat it. Finally, forget it. Move on. Don't let the mistake lodge in your memory bank.

My coach reminded us players that the best athletes in the world are amnesiacs. They quickly forget the last play. It's finished. There is nothing you can do to change it. The most important play or shot in any game is the next one.

Ultimately, my dad and college basketball coach were teaching me the importance of perseverance. These were among the most valuable lessons I have ever learned. Over the course of my life, I have experienced several difficult, gut-wrenching times that sucker-punched my insides. I never saw them coming, and I didn't know if I could continue. I wouldn't want any person to go through them. They happened, just like Dad warned me.

How did I conquer these circumstances and keep moving forward? Perseverance. That is what enabled me to conquer the trials and experience a new power from God. I hated going through those situations. But in the end, I became grateful for all I learned from them. God breathed a new perspective of his eternal grace into my heart because of them.

Great leaders all agree that perseverance is an essential trait for achieving success. And perseverance is what we as parents must ingrain into our children so that they can succeed in life.

Some leaders suggest that more and more children today are lacking the needed trait of perseverance. For example, Mitch Daniels, the head of Purdue University, wrote an article titled, "Let's Value Grit over Grades."[19] He addressed the continued debate that has arisen among educators regarding which is more important: grades or perseverance?

Recently, some colleges announced that they will not demand that applicants provide standardized test scores. In the future, they will examine only high school grade-point averages and certain types of subjective information.

In the article, Daniels said that Purdue University will not join this group. He argued that admission criteria that ignores either the SAT or ACT exam results cannot accurately predict whether a student can be successful in college. When these are not examined, it's impossible to place freshmen students in the right courses. It does the student a disservice and risks an avoidable failure.

Daniels also argued for the need to look at a student's GPA and standardized test scores. Together, they give a reliable indicator of whether a student is able to persevere. Only by exercising some kind of ongoing discipline in their academics could they have received a good test score and GPA.

Can a high GPA alone give evidence of a student's ability to persevere? Maybe, maybe not. Too many schoolteachers inflate grades these days. How does a college admissions office know which grades can be believed?

Last year, researchers found that almost half of all high school seniors had an *A* average. In 1998, only 38.9 percent of seniors got an *A* average. Evidently, more students are getting higher marks. Top students are given extra credit to boost their GPA and help them prepare for more strenuous academic rigors. Today, a 4.0 GPA is not as unusual as it used to be.

Here is the dilemma for college admissions offices: Is the student successful because of perseverance or lax grading? Does a student have grit, or did he or she receive a gift from the teacher? If it's the later, then sloth has replaced determination. And that's not good for anyone—student or institution alike.

The same problem exists today for corporations that recruit kids fresh out of college. Does a student have what it takes to do well? Can the potential employee withstand the rigors of the contemporary work environment? That's one reason many corporations and companies like to hire college athletes. They know that athletes are disciplined. They have learned the difficult challenge of balancing both academics and athletics. In this way, they have proven themselves.

Daniels went on to write,

> The emotional fragility of many young people today is, by now, a well-documented phenomenon. College students' psychological problems, and genuine mental illness, are very real; every school I know of approaches the matter with utter seriousness and responsibility. Running a college necessitates ever-growing numbers of counselors and therapists, but keeping up can be difficult.[20]

The problems kids are experiencing today are real. No one denies that. They do feel loneliness and academic anxiety. Some experience cyberbullying as well.

But as we said earlier, when parents overprotect their children, the result can be anxiety. We cannot help but wonder if the fact that parents are prone to overprotect their children is a factor in their anxieties. Then when life knocks them down, they don't know how to get up.

If we constantly give participation trophies to all the children, they will never face the pain of defeat and learn from it. They will not know how to succeed amid trials and adversity.

Today's children seem to depend on counseling and the growing therapeutic culture to answer life's challenges. Might that be hurting them?

Daniels suggested that we rename the GPA to mean the "Grit Potential Assessment" so that we are mindful of whether college applicants have the trait of perseverance, which is needed to succeed in college. If we had such an assessment tool, he guaranteed that he would be the first customer to use it.

If we don't learn the importance of facing and dealing with difficulties, we won't learn perseverance. That principle is affirmed in Scripture:

> Count it all joy, my brothers, when you meet trials of various kinds, for you know that the testing of your faith produces steadfastness. And let steadfastness have its full effect, that you may be perfect and complete, lacking in nothing (James 1:2-3).

What Is Most Important

We as parents need to ask whether we are teaching our children how to persevere. Or are we increasing the likelihood that they will become worriers? Are we part of the problem?

If we have not taught our kids how to persevere, the first step is to repent, to change, to move in another direction. To do that, you must possess an unabashed, yielded faith in Jesus.

Ask yourself the following questions: Is Jesus the master passion of your life? Do you trust him in every area? When you are tempted to worry, do your kids see you pray? Do they see you cast all your cares upon the Lord? Do you give the situation entirely to God? And believe that he alone is able to carry your burden and use it for your good and his glory?

Or do you worry?

Here is how my wife Marilynn and I tried to prevent the curse of worry from affecting our children: We tried to live out our faith in Jesus before them. When life's trials crashed upon us, we wanted our kids to see us praying, not fretting. We desired for them to see us looking to God's Word for answers, not the world.

Marilynn and I also made sure to confront any fear we saw in their lives. We were relentless and unyielding about this. We would not permit fear to enter our home or affect our thoughts. Rather, we identified our fears, gave them over to God, and let him handle them.

Your children will see and know whether you have surrendered your all to Jesus. They can ascertain whether fear or faith rules your heart. They will know whether you are walking by faith or sight.

> ## Build faith in your kids by living your faith before them.

If you have a deep, abiding faith in Jesus, most likely your children will as well. If your kids see you persevering in faith through a tough trial, they will learn how to follow suit when a difficult situation comes their way.

Your kids are likely to imitate you. They are going to watch your example for guidance on how to live. Are you a living Bible that bolsters their faith, one they can read and obey?

Build faith in your kids by living your faith before them. Let them see that you have been transformed by the renewing of your mind (Romans 12:2). Explain to them what it means to take every thought captive (2 Corinthians 10:5). Show them, by word and deed, how you do not allow fear-filled and anxiety-laden thoughts to take hold in your mind.

Demonstrate to your kids that you are allergic to anxiety and live in complete faith in Jesus. Help your children see that you are absolutely convinced that he is the sovereign Lord of the universe…and your life.

Their eyes are watching you. Give them a reason to want your faith in Jesus—especially in tough times. Your example will be of immeasurable help to them *when,* not if, difficult trials come their way.

Final Thoughts

If your children see you worrying, they will follow your example. Your worry will become theirs.

If you don't teach your kids how to persevere through difficult experiences, they will never learn how to become more than a conqueror (Romans 8:37). Instead, they will develop a victim mentality. They will blame others. And worry will be an everyday struggle.

Teach your children well! Be honest about the world's difficulties without creating worry. Teach your kids the power of perseverance. Model for them how to live a fearless life.

This is within your reach because Jesus has already overcome the power of sin, death, hell, and the devil. His resurrection power lives in those of us who believe (Romans 8:11). As his follower, you possess this same overcoming power. Use it. And make sure your kids are able to witness it in you.

Jesus is the way, the truth, and the life (John 14:6). He came to give us life and give it to us abundantly (John 10:10). He is the bread of life who sustains us (John 6:35). He is the light of the world, the One who overcomes the danger of darkness (John 8:12). He lights the path before us so that we know where to take our next step (Psalm 119:105). When we abide in him, trusting him with every area of our lives, we will know the truth, and it will set us free (John 8:32).

Do you believe this? If so, that can be the healing balm your children need for their anxieties.

Decide today that as for you and your house, you will totally follow the Lord (Joshua 24:15).

Determine that faith, not fear, will rule your home.

Your children are watching.

NOTES

1. Adam Hamilton, "Fear Is Gripping More People in the Church," *ChurchLeaders*, March 21, 2018, https://churchleaders.com/outreach-missions/outreach-missions-articles/321440-churchgoers-and-fear.html.

2. Jeffrey M. Jones, "U.S. Concerns About Healthcare High; Energy, Unemployment Low," *Gallup*, March 26, 2018, https://news.gallup.com/poll/231533/concerns-healthcare-high-energy-unemployment-low.aspx.

3. Amy Morin, "Loneliness Is as Lethal as Smoking 15 Cigarettes Per Day. Here's What You Can Do About It," *Inc.*, June 18, 2018, https://www.inc.com/amy-morin/americas-loneliness-epidemic-is-more-lethal-than-smoking-heres-what-you-can-do-to-combat-isolation.html.

4. "UK Appoints a Minister of Loneliness," *New York Times*, January 17, 2018, https://www.nytimes.com/2018/01/17/world/europe/uk-britain-loneliness.html.

5. Amy Morin, "Why the Internet Has Made Us Lonelier Than Ever," *Psychology Today*, October 19, 2018, https://www.psychologytoday.com/us/blog/what-mentally-strong-people-dont-do/201810/why-the-internet-has-made-us-lonelier-ever.

6. Margaux Masten, "The Damage Social Media Does on Empathy," *Feeling Good*, October 20, 2016, http://blogs.rochester.edu/feelinggood1/2016/10/20/the-damage-social-media-does-on-empathy/.

7. "Question: A 2014 Pew Study Found That the Average US Facebook…," *Chegg Study*, https://www.chegg.com/homework-help/questions-and-answers/2014-pew-study-found-average-us-facebook-user-338-friends-study-also-found-median-us-faceb-q23924578

8. "Americans check their phones 80 times a day: study," *New York Post*, November 8, 2017, https://nypost.com/2017/11/08/americans-check-their-phones-80-times-a-day-study/.

9. Justin McCarthy, "Trust in Government to Protect Against Terrorism at New Low," *Gallup*, December 11, 2015, https://news.gallup.com/poll/187622/trust-government-protect-against-terrorism-new-low.aspx?g_source=Politics&g_medium=newsfeed&g_campaign=tiles.

10. Jeffrey M. Jones, "U.S. Concerns About Healthcare High; Energy, Unemployment Low."

11. Mary Kate Hogan, "Closet Envy," *This Old House*, https://www.magzter.com/articles/12422/263218/5a9544b763a4c/.

12. Hogan, "Closet Envy."

13. Stephen Hawking, *A Brief History of Time* (New York: Bantam, 1998), 190.

14. Gregory Benford, "Leaping the Abyss: Stephen Hawking on Black Holes, Unified Field Theory and Marilyn Monroe," *Reason*, April 2002, 29, https://reason.com/2002/04/01/leaping-the-abyss-2/.

15. "Science says gig-going can help you live longer and increases wellbeing," *O2*, March 27, 2018, https://news.o2.co.uk/press-release/science-says-gig-going-can-help-you-live-longer-and-increases-wellbeing/.

16. Kendra Cherry, "10 Surprising Psychological Benefits of Music," updated April 6, 2019, *very wellmind*, https://www.verywellmind.com/surprising-psychological-benefits-of-music-4126866.

17. David Platt on Twitter, March 23, 2019.

18. Megan McArdle, "How did America end up raising Generation Paranoia?," *The Washington Post*, November 13, 2018, https://www.washingtonpost.com/opinions/how-did-america-end-up-raising-generation-paranoia/2018/11/13/5d294ec8-e78b-11e8-b8dc-66cca409c180_story.html?noredirect=on.

19. Mitch Daniels, "Let's Value Grit over Grades," *The Washington Post*, November 30, 2018, https://www.sltrib.com/opinion/commentary/2018/11/30/mitch-daniels-lets-value/.

20. Daniels, "Let's Value Grit over Grades."

OTHER GREAT HARVEST HOUSE BOOKS BY DAVID AND MARILYNN CHADWICK

Hearing the Voice of God
David Chadwick

Each entry in this book begins with an assigned reading from the book of John, followed by a key passage for the day, and concludes with an encouraging insight and devotion. As you ponder and apply what you learn, you'll begin to hear God speaking powerfully and personally through his Word and become more attuned to his voice in all of Scripture.

It's How You Play the Game
David Chadwick

Dean Smith won 879 games during his legendary career as a basketball coach. He also won the respect and admiration of those who worked and played for him. What set him apart and made him so effective as a leader? You'll discover 12 principles that marked Smith's approach to leadership and learn what it takes to play the game well…and win.

From Superficial to Significant
David Chadwick

You know success looks different to God than it does to the world. But in what ways? What should you know, believe, and do in order to pursue the kind of greatness that pleases God? Pastor Chadwick looks at what it means to live a remarkable Christian life—to grow your faith, make sure you know what it really means to be great in God's eyes.

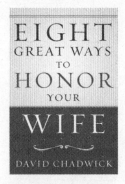

Eight Great Ways to Honor Your Wife
David Chadwick

God calls you not only to love your wife, but also to honor her—this will take your marriage to a whole new level. Join author David Chadwick as he shares eight great ways to make honoring your wife an everyday part of your life.